Reuben B. Scott

The History of the 67th Regiment Indiana Infantry Volunteers

War of the Rebellion

Reuben B. Scott

The History of the 67th Regiment Indiana Infantry Volunteers
War of the Rebellion

ISBN/EAN: 9783337116460

Printed in Europe, USA, Canada, Australia, Japan

Cover: Foto ©ninafisch / pixelio.de

More available books at **www.hansebooks.com**

THE HISTORY

—OF THE—

67th REGIMENT

Indiana : Infantry : Volunteers,

War of the Rebellion.

———0———

BEDFORD, INDIANA:
HERALD BOOK AND JOB PRINT.
1892.

PREFACE.

Lest the patriotic deeds and sufferings of silent heroes be forgotten in the debris of the dead past I am induced to pen the lines of the following pages.

In compiling this work we found that to record all personal reminiscences would make a work too voluminous for the work, hence we have avoided personal mention and adhered to the main thread of our historic story whose details as to facts are true, though slight errors in dates may occur. To the great battles that the regiment was engaged in we have only attempted to give a slight description of the immediate locality of our regiment and many of the engagements as recorded in the list of "Battles of the Rebellion," and as set forth in the list in this work has not received a description since in the stirring times of this great conflict we fought many skirmishes that in former wars would have been called battles, and are now recorded in the War Department as such, though we took but little account of at the time. From the fact that we were twice captured by the enemy, and our papers and records destroyed, reports are necessarily incomplete, and it is not claimed that this work is absolutely correct in every particular, but as an historic fact it is true and as such is submitted to the survivors of the regiment and to the general public and is

DEDICATED TO YOUNG AMERICA BY

R. B. SCOTT.

CHAPTER I.

ORGANIZATION—BATTLE OF MUMFORDSVILLE, KY.—TAKEN PRISONERS OF WAR—RETURN TO INDIANAPOLIS.

> O, war is cruel hearted! Ay, the man
> That in the private walks of life was kind,
> Even to the nursing mother's tender fears;
> Who started at a funeral knell and walked
> With slow, sad step and sympathizing eye
> When the hearse passed with one he never knew—
> Why, he, when war's stern strength is in his soul,
> Will stalk in apathy o'er slaughtered friends,
> Counting the dead and dying, as their loss
> Was all computed in the numerous slain.
> —MRS. HOLES ORMOND GROSVENOR.

The Sixty-seventh Regiment Indiana Volunteers was organized in the Third Congressional District by companies raised in the following counties, viz: One from Owen and Monroe, two from Lawrence, four from Jackson, one from Bartholomew, one from Jennings and one from Jefferson, rendezvousing at Madison about the middle of August, 1862.

This regiment was organized with the field and line officers and men as set forth in the succeeding tabulated pages, and whose average age was twenty years; boys who, when the war-cloud burst forth in cyclones of fire and battle, dropped their school books, laid down their farming tools, came from workshops and stores, and rushed, at their country's call, to Madison, and on the 19th and 20th of August, 1862, by companies held up their hands toward heaven and in the presence of Almighty God swore allegiance to the United States, and to defend it against all its enemies of whatever nature, and to obey our superior officers who might be appointed over us.

Then for the first time in our lives we erected and inhabited a convass city of the United States, situated just below the city in a nice beech grove whose shades protected us from the burning rays of the August sun, while we went through the novelties of preparing for active warfare by drawing new United States uniforms, some of which were too long at one end, while others were too short at both. This difficulty was soon satisfactorily overcome by the long boys swapping with the short boys, and thus those thousand boys from all vocations and every walk of life were now all dressed up in United States uniforms and as proud as little boys with their first pantaloons.

Having all been satisfactorily uniformed we formed in line by companies and tried to march—which was new, novel and awkward to us—up to the ordnance tent where each of us drew a great, big new Belgium rifle having a long cutlass to fasten upon the muzzle. Then came cartridge boxes and belts the like of which we had never seen; and when, after many difficulties, we were all rigged out in *armour de war* when we again fell in line with guns in hand and we were now on the war-path snapping our guns and filling the air with the tune of rattling ramrods as we marched to our quarters, where we made an attempt to stack arms. Scarcely had we lain off our armor when we were again called into line, when we began to ask ourselves, "When would this thing end?" as we marched up to the quartermaster's tent, where we drew a gum puncho, a wool blanket and a wardrobe in the shape of a knapsack and finally a canteen, which finished the list of our complete outfit, and we felt ourselves now ready for active warfare.

We had but little time to wait for action as Uncle Sam had urgent need of us, and on the 21st we received orders to strike tents, pack knapsacks, and prepare to march. Whatever this order meant we had yet to learn. However, we pulled down tents, and after many difficulties managed to put our things in our knapsacks and succeeded in strapping them upon our backs, and with accoutrements and gun, making a load of about 60 pounds weight, we managed to get into line as a regiment, for the first time, and mercy on us! do they expect us to march and fight with this ungodly load strapped upon our backs? This question was subsequently answered to our satisfaction. Colonel Emerson now gave the order and we moved out and down to the wharf where we embarked upon a steamboat amid rousing patriotic cheers from on board which seemed to echo from hill to hill and to be caught up by the rippling waters below, and answered back by the waving of 'kerchiefs and throwing of kisses by the citizens and ladies on shore, filling the very air with patriotism as we shoved off from the Hoosier shore some of us never to return.

We moved down the river, enjoying the nice scenery as the evening passed. When we arrived at Louisville, Ky., we debarked and went into camp near the L. & N. railroad depot, where we remained but a few days, besieged by peddlers and hucksters, who seemed to avail themselves of our inexperience; but we were soon ordered to fall in and march to the depot, where we boarded box cars and steamed southward. After a few hours we arrived at Mumfordsville, Ky., where we stopped and went into camp on the left of the railroad, and on looking about we found fragments of the Seventeenth and Fiftieth Indiana regiments and one company of the Fifty-fourth and the Eighty-ninth Indiana, who had preceded us a few days, and a few United States Regulars. On our right was a small stockade in which was one small piece of artillery. From this stockade, in a crescent, extended a line of breastworks around to the extreme left, where it terminated in a fort, in which was a section of small guns. Inside of these crescent-shaped works were placed the aforenamed troops, amounting in all to about 2,600, with something over 2,000 small arms.

We were now in the enemy's country, without drill or discipline, liable to be attacked at any time, making it imperative that we should enter upon our military education at once. So Corporal Richardson, of Company C, having received some instruction as to the steps and facings, was ordered to take us out and drill us in squad drill. This proved very amusing to him, as well as laborious and awkward to us, being a laughable scene to the lookers on.

Our first picket duty came here when we had to be placed away out from camp in little squads, to keep watch while the rest of the camp slept, which now began to wear all the novelty off of soldier life, but all went on well, as the general routine of camp life was being performed from day to day, until late in the evening of the 12th, when a company or two were ordered to fall in with guns and cartridge boxes, and were marched down to the railroad where, just at dark, we boarded a train of flat cars and were ordered to lay down flat on our stomachs, which, with a serious questioning, we did, while we steamed south over a rough road which tried the endurance and elasticity of our stomachs while we sped along through the darkness expecting at any moment to be fired into by some ambushed enemy ; but nothing exciting occurring, we arrived at Bowling Green after a few hours horizontal riding. Here we loaded up our train with provisions and returned before morning. This new departure created a suspicion in our minds that the Rebels were near. On the 13th our suspicions were strengthened by seeing active preparations for and precautions against an attack, and when we saw officers in little groups conversing in undertones, we knew trouble was pending ; and when late in the evening, while the sun was setting beneath the western horison, sending a great halo of glory up the western sky, and the soft, dusky curtain of twilight in columns began to draw about us, in slow and measured tread, in silence companies were moving out and strengthening the picket line, and after being placed in lines, settled down with gun in hand to await the coming events.

The dark, still night was slowly passing away, when, near twelve o'clock, a flag of truce came slowly up and demanded a surrender of the forts and forces, which General

Wilder refuses, and after some parleying they return and again the whole line settled into silence and suspense, while General Wilder places his troops in position for defense by putting the Eighty-ninth Indiana over on the right and the Sixty-seventh on the left, while the fragments of regulars were placed on different points along the line. Now, all being placed in readiness to receive the enemy, the great rows of uniformed Hoosiers, just from the church and schoolroom, with guns in hand, lay waiting the coming conflict, while the stars of heaven marked the passing hours.

On that Sunday morning, September 14th, in the calmness of the hour, great gray streaks of the mornings dawn began to appear in the east and shoot their silver threads of light across the blue fields of heaven, and the dew drops, from the leafy boughs began to fall and beat the reveille of early morn, and the redbird began to chirp and tune for his morning song, when suddenly, "BOOM" goes a cannon over in our front and a shell goes screeching through the air, leaving a brilliant meteoric streak of fire in its wake. Suddenly we were upon our feet and ready for action. We had never heard the boom of a cannon or screech of a shell, but we instinctively knew this to be a signal gun, and that the Rebels would soon be upon us, and a tremor of dread passes through our nerves and a pallor comes upon our cheeks, and with compressed lips and the stamp of determination upon our features we wait in silence but a few moments, when another boom, then another, then a musket quickly followed by others, and our pickets were fired upon and the rattle of musketry is heard all along the line, while the whole Rebel line is advancing. Our pickets fire and fall back in line with the skirmishers. We hear the skirmishers of the Eighty-ninth rattling away; our line is being driven in, firing and falling back, leaving their dead and wounded behind, while the Rebel hosts still press on until we are all driven into the forts and behind the breastworks, when a partial calm ensues while Rebel batteries are whirling around into position and we hear our little field pieces over on the right pounding away. Then ours on the left are making it warm for the Reb's. when the whole Rebel force, in three lines of battle, advance upon us, when instantly our whole crescent line of works were one blaze of musketry. sending deadly missiles into the Rebel ranks, whose batteries and muskets are sending a torrent of shot and shell over our heads, while with maddening yell they charge upon us, but our deadly aim has thinned their ranks, they waver and fall back, while our boys fill the air with cheers while they pour the shot into the ranks of the retreating foe. The firing has slackened, the Rebels are reforming their columns. A Rebel gun is galloped to the hill in our rear, and is about to fire upon us, when our piece is whirled around and aimed, and sends a shot that dismounts it and we have no trouble from the rear; but in front they are yelling and coming on another charge, when Major Ablott mounts the parapet and cries out : "Shoot low," when a shot strikes him and he falls dead, while on they come in a maddening rush to death, while our boys, "Hoosier squirrel hunt drill," are thinning their ranks and they again waver and fall back. Our boys fill the air with deadly missiles and a "Hoosier yell, which is echoed by the Eighty-ninth boys, when another partial calm comes, which lasts but a few minutes when the Rebel lines fetch a demoniacal yell and with glittering bayonets come on a third time on their march to death, beneath a cloud of smoke. We see a host of soldiers coming up in our rear; we wheel our cannon and bring our guns to bear upon them, when to our joy, to the soft breezes the star-spangled banner unfurls, and the old Fiftieth Indiana is coming to our aid. But on comes the Rebel host, yelling and firing, but our squirrel hunt aim is thinning their ranks and again they weaken and fall back out of rifle shot and calm is all along the line when we see a flag of truce coming up. Wilder meets it. They want to care for their wounded and bury their dead ; and thus ended the fight on Sunday morning, September 14, 1862.

BATTLE OF MUNFORDSVILLE, KY., SEPT. 14, 1862.

Our 2,200 men had withstood the storm of General Chalmers' whole division of well drilled and disciplined troops and lost forty-seven killed and wounded, while the enemy's loss was about 750; and Chalmers falls back to await the coming of Bragg's whole army.

The severity of this engagement is attested by our flag and staff being struck one hundred and forty-six times.

We occupied the remainder of the day in caring for our wounded and burying our dead, and this was one of the most horrible sights we had ever witnessed; not being inured to the horrors of battle. It seemed to us horrible to see our schoolmates of a few weeks before, now one by one laid away in the cold grave far away from home and friends.

On the next day we lay in readiness for battle, all day expecting the enemy to return and renew the attack, but he did not appear until Tuesday, the 16th, when skirmishing again commenced and continued all day. General Bragg's whole force had come up, and while the skirmishing was going on he was placing his batteries in position all around us in such a manner as to open a concentrated fire upon us.

Having his batteries so arranged, late in the evening he sends in a flag of truce and demands a surrender, which General Wilder refused, unless permitted to see for himself that he (Bragg) had the necessary troops to enforce the demand. This permission being granted, General Wilder rode around the place and counted 66 cannon, 54 of which were then in position, and was told by Bragg that there were 35,600 troops in position, which convinced him that it would be a foolish sacrifice of life to hold out longer, and Wednesday morning, September 17, we were surrendered prisoners of war.

On the 18th we were marched out by regiments and with three days' rations, by company parolled and started southward to meet General Buell and his army, who had, we hoped would come to our rescue before we were compelled to surrender.

After travelling several miles we came up to Buell's army

and remained with them one day, and then went to Bowling Green, Ky., remaining there but a little while when we started northward towards Hoosierdom, marching by day and laying up at night, until September 26, when we reached Brandenburg, and the following day crossed the river and reached New Albany, Ind., on the 27th. Here Governor Morton met us and spoke a word of cheer and encouragement to us and ordered us by rail to Indianapolis, arriving there on the 31st of September.

On the following morning we received a furlough of twenty days, which was extended seven days more. Thus within a few short weeks, we had left our harvest fields, workshops and been transformed from citizens to soldiers and been baptised in the fire of blood and battle, made prisoners of war and hungry and footsore marched one hundred and fifty miles, and now we have a little rest at home among friends.

CHAPTER II.

RETURN TO PAROLE CAMP—START SOUTHWARD—BATTLES OF CHICKASAW, BAYOU AND ARKANSAS POST.

> A thousand glorious actions that might claim
> Triumphant laurels and immortal fame,
> Confused in clouds of glorious actions lie,
> And troops of heroes undistinguished die.

While we were home on this twenty-seven day's furlough the storm clouds of late autumn had come and wintry blasts had covered mother earth beneath a blanket of snow, making it anything but inviting for us to turn out of our soft beds and leave our warm and comfortable firesides and again enter the arena of war, but such must needs be, and on the 27th of October we assembled in parole camp in Camp Morton where we again went through the process of drawing tents, blankets, clothing and knapsacks and were soon rigged up in comfortable quarters again and resumed a quiet camp life while awaiting our exchange; and to make our tents more comfortable some of us bought sheet iron stoves and placed them beneath our ground floor, having the flue to come up just outside the gable end of our tents. This proved to be quite a luxury, which we were not destined to enjoy but a brief time. As the winter drew on and the nights long and cold, our supply of wood ran short, when the whole camp became restless. So one cold night, as much through pure devilment as the want of wood, we made a raid upon the fence about us, making considerable racket which brought General McMahan out, who ordered a battery round in front and the One Hundredth Indiana to drive us into our tents. As the General was riding through camp some one bounced a club off of him, and by accident one of the One Hundredth boys got shot, from the effects of which I afterward learned, he died. But after a brief storm all was restored to order and quiet, and on the following morning our wood-pile was replenished and we had no more trouble. All was going on smoothly, when to our joy we received news of our exchange, and that we would soon be sent to the front. So on the following morning we formed in ranks by company and marched up to the ordnance department and drew our guns, this time Enfield rifles, a decided improvement upon the old Belgiums, being much neater and lighter.

We were now again ready for active duty, and were at once put upon company drills, reviews and other duties incident to the preparing us for active service, and from day to day we were put through those various evolutions necessary to inure us to the hardships of war.

While we were thus learning the art of war, the measles, to the extent almost, of an epidemic, broke out among our boys, rendering many unable for duty when on December 5, we broke camp and marched down and boarded a freight train on the Vandalia Line and steamed westward as the sun sank and the cold wintry night drew on, and as we had no way of warming ourselves we drew our blankets about us and huddled together, suffering considerable from cold as we passed through the bleak prairies of Illinois.

On the following morning we arrived at Cairo, Ill., where, eager to limber up our cramped limbs and to warm up our chilly blood, we debarked from the train and proceeded to take in the sights of the city, as well as a good warm dinner, after which we moved down to the wharf and boarded a steamer which lay there in waiting, and when all were quartered and in readiness we shoved off and headed down the great **Mississippi**.

We had heard of the great Mississippi, and in our school geographies had seen it marked off, but this was our first view of the great river, with which our subsequent history is to be so closely associated, and as our boat, by great throbs, was pushing her way down this stream, we were taking in the scenery along its banks, when the cold gray evening faded into night, whose dark curtain shut off the scene, and the night settled into silence upon river and shore, and nothing was heard in the silence of the hour except the great throbs of our engine below and the hum of voices on board.

Becoming weary we prepared for the night by wrapping ourselves in our blankets and lay upon the decks, all folded up like so many soup spoons. we lay upon one side until our very hip bones seemed to be boring holes into the deck floors. when, all being ready, the order was given to "Prepare to spoon—spoon," when the whole line at once would roll over on its other side. This was *circumstantial, voluntary* drill.

So passed the hours, and the morning came and we still kept onward to Dixie down the murky stream, and after breakfasting on hard tack and cold boiled pork we proceeded to take in the scenery along the shores, and as we were getting further south all the time we could set upon deck and enjoy the passing scenery without much discomfort, while the day waned into night and the *spoon-drill* is again performed, and so went the time night and day, and day and night, for four nights and three days, until we arrived at Memphis, Tenn., where we were again glad to be relieved from our cramped quarters. Here we debarked and went into camp up in the rear of the city, where we found a very pleasant place to camp, but wood being a little scarce we soon adopted the rule of "taking the top rail of the fencing," and we lived strictly up to this rule then; and thereafter none of the boys were ever known to take any but the "top rail."

Here we did the regular camp and picket duty and practiced target shooting and drilling company drill, and when off duty we took in the city, where we saw more "niggers" and dogs than at any place we had ever seen, and it was a disputable question as to which were in the majority—niggers, dogs or Rebels. This question is yet unsettled.

We remained here until the 20th, when we broke camp and marched down to the wharf, where we boarded the steamer "J. S. Pringle," which was one of the boats that formed the fleet that bore Sherman's gallant army to Vicksburg.

One by one, as fast as loaded, they would drop out in the stream and take position in line of order, and when they were all in line it was a grand sight to see this grand fleet loaded down to the guards with proud western troops, all in line ; as it were, a flock of huge marine birds, all decorated with floating state banners and the flag of the Union proudly waving, while the great voices of brass bands were filling the air with sweet strains of patriotic music, wafted by the breeze from shore to shore, while the muddy waves below seemed to flap and dance in gleeful harmony.

When the last strain of this music had died away and while the rippling waves were dancing, and a calm seemed to settle upon the scene, when from Sherman's headquarters boat burst forth three long and loud whistles, which were echoed by each boat in turn. The signal is given and the fleet moves off amid long and loud patriotic cheers from ten thousand loyal throats.

We move slowly and grandly down stream, now in a long stretch of the river, then rounding the curves ; as it were, passing in review, while we are taking in the scenery on the banks until night's dingy curtain shuts off the scene and we prepare to rest while our gallant fleet, through the dark hours, throbs and puffs beneath its precious load.

Next morning found us near Helena, Ark., where we had stopped for a while and received three or more boats into our fleet, when we again resumed our southward course. But as we were getting far out into Rebeldom, more caution was exercised by placing gunboats in front, which moved on down cautiously, we following closely in their wake, when on the morning of the 24th we reached Miliken's Bend, La.

Here our brigade, consisting of the Eighty-third and Ninety-sixth Ohio, Twenty-third Wisconsin and the Sixtieth and Sixty-seventh Indiana, under command of General Burbridge, debarked in light marching order moved out on quick time and kept moving hour after hour, over muddy roads, and wading sloughs until night found us near a station on the Vicksburg and Shrevesport railroad, where we found a bridge and two long trestles, which we destroyed, working nearly all night. When morning came our little field pieces sent a few shots into Rebeldom and we started on the return march.

During the night it rained, wetting our blankets and clothing and making the roads muddy, rendering it very laborious marching; but, tired and worn out as we were, beneath our wet blankets and clothing we kept marching regardless of the elements, but many were now giving out and falling by the wayside. While the main body reached the boat late in the evening, many did not come up 'till the sun had set. When all were up we re-embarked. Having been cramped up on the boat four days and nights we then disembarked and marched on quick time all day, and working all night, returned next day, having marched sixty-five miles and torn up one bridge and two trestles inside of thirty-five hours.

While we were on this march the main army remained upon their boats and when we returned and had re-embarked, on the morning of the 26th the whole fleet, preceded by gunboats, moved across the river and up the Yazoo river, the water of which was dark blue and very pretty compared to that of the Mississippi, being a temptation to the boys to fill their canteens with this pretty clear water. But we had learned that this water was poison—the word "Yazoo" in the Indian language meaning poison—and therefore refrained from filling our canteens, but many of the boys drank of this water and afterwards broke out in ulcerous sores.

We proceeded cautiously up the Yazoo, the gunboats leading the van, until we reached a point some twelve miles up the river opposite Haynes Bluff, where we halted and debarked upon a level bottom having a few cleared fields near the river. The greater portion was one great and almost interminable cypress swamp filled with bayous, swamps and cypress knees.

This level bottom extended up to the bluffs at the base of which ran a sluggish bayou. After debarking we formed by regiments and marched out and formed line of battle upon the banks of this Bayou Chickasaw, our regiment being on the extreme right.

On the opposite bank of this stream, in the swamp and underbrush, were the Rebel pickets and skirmish line, while to their rear and upon the bluffs some three hundred feet high, were placed their batteries in such a position as to make it very difficult for an army to cross this bayou and charge the hills.

Immediately upon our arrival there skirmishing and picket firing commenced across this bayou. This firing was kept up until night, when great thick walls of darkness hemmed us in and all settled down into silence and gloom. Without fire or coffee we lay ourselves down by the roots of the tall cypress trees to pass the night, while the wintry winds moaned a tune of loneliness above us.

But we had scarcely bivouaced for the night when the heavy lowering clouds that had been hanging over and above us all day now, as it were, to improve the opportunity, turned loose upon us their pent up stores of chilly waters, which poured down during the night's dungeon darkness and loneliness, and there being no way to protect ourselves we nestled beneath our oil blankets as best we could, while the patter of the rain drops marked the passing moments until the long looked for morning came and hot coffee was brought up from the rear. That warm coffee! That hot coffee! That lifegiving coffee, the soldier's delight, came. This coffee and a little exercise warmed up our benumbed limbs and firing was the order of the day, growing into fierce battles on our left while shells kept us interested by crashing among the cypress tops and dropping among us.

So, desultry firing, growing into fierce battle on the left, continued all day and when night came it found us as the night before, except that our clothing and blankets were all wet, making it very uncomfortable for us; but there is no circumstance that can prevent a wornout soldier from sleeping when his duty permits him.

After passing the long, weary night, upon the cold ground—without fire—morning was welcomed, and again hot coffee was brought up and the proceedings of the day before were repeated, except that a fierce charge on our left was made in attempting to cross the bayou, but failed with great loss. Night came again, and like the previous nights, we prepared to pass the night as before, when, in the stillness of the hour, feeling their way, came orderlies who, in whispers, gave orders to be ready to march at once. Wheels of artillery were muffled, wagon and ambulance wheels were wrapped in blankets, and while the heavy fogs hung around like great misty curtains, while darkness screened our movements from the enemy's view, we moved out as silent as a funeral procession and marched to the boats, upon which we soon embarked and moved down the river, while the gunboats gave the Rebels a few farewell shots, and followed.

This retreat was on December 31st, and on the 1st of January, 1863, found us near the mouth of the Yazoo, and from there, on the 2d, we moved up to Miliken's Bend; we having been engaged three days and nights in skirmishing and fighting, suffering severely from the cold, wintry rains, and finally, at dead hour of night, had to retreat and leave the enemy in his stronghold.

When we left Memphis, Tenn.—on December 20th—it was understood by Generals Grant and Sherman that Grant should take his army and proceed via Holly Springs and Grenada and come upon Vicksburg in the rear; while Sherman should take his army down the Mississippi and up the

Yazoo and attack at Hayne's Bluff, or Chickasaw Bayou. To this latter place we had gone, and after fighting three days and nights, a courier came through and informed Sherman that Van Dorn had threatened Grant's base of supplies, compelling him to fall back on Memphis, leaving Pemberton's whole army free to pounce upon us at once, hence this retreat.

When we arrived at Miliken's Bend, we found that General John A. McClenard had arrived from up the river with papers to supersede General Sherman, and in so doing, divided the army into two corps, the one to be commanded by General Sherman and the other by General Geo. W. Morgan while McClenard commanded the whole. We were assigned to Sherman's corps.

Owing to some having contracted measles while at Indianapolis, and to our late extreme exposure during our Hayne's Bluff expedition, many of the boys were falling sick and unable for duty by reason of measles, pneumonia and camp diarrhœa.

While lying here, on board of our vessels, we were all curious to know where next we would go, or what next would be undertaken. About this time the steamer, Blue Wing, on her way down with mail and supplies for the army, was captured by the Rebels near the mouth of White river, and taken up to Arkansas Post, about forty miles up the Arkansas river. This determined McClenard to at once move his whole fleet up the river, until, reaching the mouth of White river, we went up it, coming to a cut-off which let us into the Arkansas, up which we went, arriving just below Arkansas Post, or Fort Hinman, on January 10th. We landed and found a strong fort, built of earth and heavy oak timbers, doubly lined with closely-fitting railroad iron. From this fort for nearly a mile, extended heavy breastworks, in front of which was a deep ditch, partially filled with water; and inside this fort were batteries of heavy canon, and about 5,000 troops, all under the command of General Churchill.

After landing and forming in column by regiments, we moved upon a low, flat bottom, filled with mud holes and covered with logs and underbrush, rendering it exceedingly difficult to move in column, but after many difficulties, we were in line of battle about the fort and just out of rifle shot, but where the cannon could interest us by their oft-repeated messages of defiance.

Our regiment occupied a position on the left center, and after halting a little while, all the line was advanced slowly, when night came, and with it (which always seemed to be our fate) came the rain, which continued most of the night, during which our batteries were being brought around and placed in position, while Sherman was bringing troops and batteries into position on the right.

While these operations were going on, the heavy gun boats were feeling of the heavy batteries on the river front, and during the long and tedious hours of the night, while we lay there in the cold and wet we could hear the heavy boom of the guns on the boats, and could see the fiery streaks of the shells as they passed through the fields of darkness.

So wore away the night and morning came, and when the gray streaks of morn lighted up the scene about us we could see in our front that all the trees had been felled with the tops toward us and having their limbs sharpened outward, forming a thick abattis, while just beyond was a cleared space terminating at the deep ditch in front of the works.

No sooner had morning come than desultory firing was commenced all along the line, punctuated now and then by the boom of a cannon and underscored occasionally by the screeching shells while the gunboats were making it interesting on the river front and our lines were inching their way close up to the fallen trees when for a while the batteries all along the line and the gunboats on the river opened up a heavy bombardment, to which the Rebels for a while replied briskly and fiercely, when finally the bombardment ceased all along the line and a silence of a few moments ensued, when a charge was ordered. With mighty yells each one grasped his musket and sprang forward amid a torrent of minnie balls, grape and canister, rushed through the brush, over the cleared space, into the ditch and up on the bank, when white flags appeared all along the line and the fort and 5,000 prisoners were ours, while we (the Union forces) lost in this charge 977; 129 being killed, while the Sixty-seventh lost three killed and thirty-five wounded.

This fight took place on the 11th of January, and after caring for the wounded and burying the dead, we proceeded to level down the works by plunging their largest gun into a deep well, dismounting the rest and so destroying the fort and works as to render them entirely useless for the enemy.

While we were here, as usual after a battle, the floodgates of heaven seemed to be opened and the cold January rain poured down incessantly for two days and nights, when on the 14th we were ordered on board our boats.

We had paid the last sad rites that one comrade can pay to another, and the shades of darkness were spreading sable curtains about us and the tears of heaven were falling upon the mounds of the dead, and the adjacent forests were hushed in silence of mourning, while the winds among the tall cypress trees played a solemn requiem as we gave our last sad look and shed a tear for the dead, when we shoved off and headed down the river. We were wet, weary and worn out, and sought rest by wrapping our wet blankets about us and lying down in our wet clothes.

> Side by side, an hundred long,
> On both sides the boat we lay
> In one continuous weary throng,
> While the raging winds about us play.

We had scarcely entered upon our downward trip, when the wind veered around to the north and turned suddenly cold, while the air became filled with drifting snow, exposing those on the north side of the vessel to extreme suffering.

driving them to the opposite side. The boat being heavily laden, was now in danger of being toppled over, making it necessary to place a guard to keep these suffering men on their own side of the boat. But in turn, as we rounded the bends, each side received the blasts of wind and snow, and nestling down in their wet clothes beneath their wet blankets, as the hours of this terrible night passed, the snow blew and partially covered these brave boys beneath a sheet of sleet and snow, while the majestic trees on the banks bowed their heads to the solemn moan that the winds were playing over the departed dead and the suffering living.

Hour after hour we thus passed down the river until morning finally came and found us at Napoleon, Ark., when, to our joy, the winter storm cloud had passed away and the cold winds ceased to blow, and the great golden sun had arisen in his most beauteous splendor. Never in our lives were his warm rays more highly appreciated or welcomed than upon this January morning.

But what a sight! There, upon those open decks, lay those brave patriots in their wet clothes and covered with their wet blankets, which, in places, were frozen together; while the hair of some of the boys was frozen to the floor, and at other places, as it were, heaven had spread a white, winding sheet about the dead and dying.

We remained here until the 18th, when General Grant came down from Memphis and assumed command and ordered the whole fleet to Young's Point, La.

CHAPTER III.

VICKSBURG CAMPAIGN.

"Mourn not for them, the loved and gone!
The cause they died to save
Plants an eternal corner stone
Upon the martyr's grave;
And, safe from all the ills we pass,
Their sleep is sweet and low,
Neath requiems of the murmuring grass
And dirges of the snow."

On arriving at Young's Point, La., on January 21st, we embarked and went into camp just over the levee, upon a low plantation ground in a sharp bend of the river; the river forming two sides of a triangle, while bayous and swamps formed the other. In this triangle Grant camped his troops, about four miles from, and in front of Vicksburg, where we could see the great batteries placed upon the brow of the hills defending her river front.

Across this narrow neck of land, General Williams, some time prior, had sought to turn the great river away from the city, by cutting a canal across from the river above, to the river below, through which the mighty waters might flow and cut a permanent channel; but movements at other places had drawn him away, and the ditch for the time-being was abandoned. Gen. Grant, on assuming command, as per order from the War Department, organized the western army into five army corps, as follows:

The 13th, commanded by John A. McClenard.
The 14th, by George H. Morgan.
The 15th, by William Sherman.
The 16th, by Gen. Hurlbut.
The 17th, by James B. McPherson.

But the limits of our brief history will not permit us to follow all these armies; but we are compelled to confine ourselves to our own immediate brigade and regiment, we belonging to the 1st brigade, 2d division, of the 13th army corps; composed of the 83d and 96th Ohio, 23d Wisconsin, and the 60 and 67th Indiana, and as these regiments were together during the remainder of the war, from this time on the history of one becomes the history of all.

Now, Grant, after establishing his army here, saw the fast-rising waters of the river, and sought to avail himself of the circumstance, and either for employment for the army, or for practical results, again resumed the digging of the canal, and from day to day, details from companies and regiment, were put to digging in the muddy, watery ditch, and while others were digging here, our brigade was ordered on the old steamer—Maria Denning—and when all was ready, we steamed up the river all that day and night, and next day until about noon, when we reached a point just below Greenville, Miss., where we landed upon a large plantation, where we found much corn and some cattle, which we, during two days, loaded upon our boat, while forage and scouting parties scoured the country for some miles around, finding several mules with no one to care for them, hence were appropriated and turned over to the quartermaster's department; and many of the boys brought great buckets of honey, while others paid their attention to dressed pigs and fowls, until finally, the boat being pretty well loaded, all re-embarked and returned to camp, where our fresh supplies were highly appreciated by our invalids.

On returning, we resumed ordinary camp and picket duties, and all was going on smoothly without any particular excitement, when one evening, just after dark, we received orders to prepare three day's rations, and be ready to march in light marching order (with gun and wool blankets) at daylight; what we were going to do or where we were going, were some of the things unknowable by the common army.

and without question, we were ready at the appointed time, and early next morning we moved out to the landing, and boarded a steamer and headed up the river; and pressing against the current, our steamer kept puffing away and carrying her burden as fast as she could, until we reached Greenville, Miss., where we landed, and with Gen. Burbridge at our head, set out for the interior on a fast march; but we had gone but a short distance when it began to rain, and continued to rain all day, while we pushed on as fast as we could through mud and water, and coming to a large swamp—like slough—which, from the late rains was now swollen and forming almost a barrier to our further progress; but Gen. Burbridge rode through, and finding it no more than waist deep in the deepest place it was decided to wade it, and with cartridge boxes held well up, we waded through and proceeded on our muddy march, moving nearly all the evening, while the rain continued. Finally we came up to and captured a small cannon, pulled by a yoke of oxen and being near night and a fine plantation close by, seemed to invite us to stop over, which we did, occupying the dwelling, barn and nigger quarters, where we could rest, and listen to the patter of the rain-drops upon the roof.

When morning came, after breakfasting upon the luxuries of an inland plantation, with our trophy, we started back over this same muddy road, and wading the same swollen slough, and arrived at the boat late in the evening and lay there all night; and on the morning following, steamed up the river some miles, where we went into the interior, but upon finding nothing of interest, after stopping a few days, we returned to the boat and boarded her, and steamed down the river and landed at our camp, having been out fourteen days on three day's rations; and yet had plenty contributed to us by the confederacy.

During all this time the digging in the canal was going on, but it was becoming difficult work, as the rain from above and the water around them, kept filling it with water; and now, as the winter was receding before spring, and the clouds had been over us for weeks, were now turning loose upon us their great fountains, in torrents of incessant rain, and from day to day and night unto night, this rain kept pouring, while the great waters in the river were rising, converting the swamps in our rear into a great lake, almost threatening to deluge us out, while our camp became one perfect quagmire of mud—in as much as to deprive us of a dry place to lay our heads—and our rations were spoiling; while our blankets and clothing were damp and mildewing, and while sickness of rheumatism, pneumonia and camp diarrhœ, had, as it were, with one fell swoop—like a scourge—smitten our camp, prostrating two hundred at one time, out of our three hundred present, making our camp a veritable hospital of the sick and dying, while the levee, the only dry spot of earth, became a burial ground of the dead.

And often, when night spread her sable curtains about us, in the still hours of the night, might be seen little groups of men, like spectres of a grave-yard, around the little green cottonwood camp-fires; and when the last pale little blaze would flicker, and, in the solemn silence, fade and go out, then their spectral forms, like spirits among the tombs, would seek his damp and mouldy couch.

About this time, Great Britain—away over the waters—was holding out encouragements of a soon recognition of the confederacy; and a secret organization, called "The Knights of the Golden Circle," a society in sympathy of the rebellion, was forming all over Indiana and Illinois and other states, discouraging enlistments and encouraging desertion from the army; and many a fair maiden, in penning a line of love to her lover, imbued it with the spirit of poison that disgraced him forever; while telling him to desert and he should be protected. All this coming to us while in the shades of sickness and death, making the darkest hours of the war.

And while the mails from home were the brightest gems of this dark period, yet some of them breathed disgrace and dishonor and shame, and caused some to desert the flag of their country, disgracing themselves before men and perjuring themselves before God.

About this time Gen. Grant moved us up to Miliken's Bend, where we found good high ground to camp on, and good dry wood to warm by and cook our rations; and the torn clouds of winter had passed away, the warm spring sun was drying up the mud, and our health began to improve, and with it, our spirits began to rise; things looked brighter, and again about this time we took another scout up the river to Boliver, Miss., and scouting around there a day or two, nothing of moment occuring, we soon returned to camp to enjoy our captured bacon and fowl.

Now, in the latter half of March, Grant commenced massing his whole army here. McPherson came down from Lake Providence, Sherman from Steele's Bayou, while Hurlbut sent all his available troops. The convalescents were all brought, and we were now drilling and preparing for a campaign, while the roads were becoming solid, and the sun and spring winds were drying up the water.

So, on the night of the 24th of March, while the thick walls of darkness secured our movements from the rebels, a gun-boat, towing two barges, ran down past the rebel batteries without loss or injury, and soon Grant ordered other transports to follow; but the crews refused to go, and when volunteers were called for from the army, a hundred would volunteer where ten would be wanted. On the 26th, these transports, accompanied by some gun-boats, ran the gauntlet of storm and iron hail and successfully passed below.

All was now in readiness for a move, and on the first day of April, our 13th army corps broke camp and marched out near to New Richmond, where we camped for the night.

While we were at Miliken's Bend, a small dram of whiskey was issued to us each morning; when we came to leave, there was a barrel of whiskey that could not be taken along, and the boys filled their canteens with whiskey instead of water.

while on the first days march, many became boisterous and funny, and at night caused considerable racket. On the following morning when all were in line ready for march, Major Seers walked out in front of the line and gave the following order: "Battalion, turn up canteens and pour out whiskey." when all along the line—guzzle, guzzle, guzzle went the whiskey, and never before or since, have we seen such an outpouring of the spirits; and we moved out slowly as leaving some dear friend.

After marching all day, night found us at Horn's plantation, where we camped upon the margin of a Bayou, and remained a few days when we moved up to Smith's plantation. During these marches, the roads were so muddy that we were compelled to march in single file, and any way to get along, while ammunition was pulled along the bayous on log rafts. We remained at Smith's plantation but a day or so, when we moved down to Bayou Videl, where a small steamer came up and we boarded her and moved down, pushing our way through the saplings and finally arrived at Perkin's plantation, some thirty-five miles below Vicksburg.

Remaining here over night, on the morrow, we moved on down the river to Hardtimes Landing, where we were met by the transports and gun-boats that ran the Vicksburg batteries on the 24 and 26 of March, and on the morning of April 29th boarded one of these steamers, while the other regiments and batteries were loaded on the other boats, and all steamed down the river some ten or twelve miles where Big Black river makes a junction with the Mississippi; making a large body of water called Grand Gulf, where the rebels had the point at the junction well fortified by rifle pits upon the brow of the hill, and heavy water batteries at the waters edge, making it a very formidable place.

Gen. Grant's orders were for the gun-boats to silence these batteries and field pieces, and for the infantry to land in the face of the enemy, and take the place by storm; and for five hours while the gun-boats were bombarding these works, we remained upon the steamer waiting our turn. Meantime, Gen Grant, on a little tug just out of reach of shot, with field-glass in hand, was inspecting the works; finally he returned to the fleet and said that the batteries could not be silenced, and we could not take it by storm; and he immediately ordered the troops to depart and march across the narrow neck of land to the river below, while the fleet and gun-boats should run past the batteries, and thus we were saved a repetition of that fruitless charge at Chickasaw bayou.

After marching across this neck to the river below, we lay down for the night, and when the morning (April 30th) had come, we mustered for pay, and again boarded a vessel and went across to Bruinsburg, in Mississippi, landing late in the evening. After unslinging our knapsacks and piling them up, leaving a guard with them, we drew three day's rations, (to do five) and in light marching order, "as the shades of the warm April evening settled upon valleys and hills," we moved in a northerly direction across the valley—towards the hills—where we struck high, dry ground, for the first time in five long weary, wet months; during which we had been marching, scouting and fighting through mud and water; wading Bayous and swamps; camping upon boggs, and sleeping in wet and mouldy blankets; while sickness death and funeral marches were daily occurances. And now, when our feet struck the solid, firm roads, it seemed to give buoyancy to our limbs and stimulate our spirits as we marched along these narrow defiles among the hills, and through the dark, over-hanging forests, of tall magnolia trees, whose sweet-scented blossoms perfumed and lent an enchantment to the cool night air, as it kissed our cheeks and cooled our brows.

We kept pushing forward, as the dark hours passed, until about two o'clock in the morning. Away in front, upon the calm night air, we heard the sound of musketry, then the boom of cannon; when hurrah! after hurrah! rang forth from our boys, making the very forest about tremble; while our steps were quickened as we, with stimulated energy, pushed on, resting a few moments now and then, as the hours sped away; and when the gray streaks of early morn drove away the darkness and lit up the hills about us, we could see the blue smoke of the night's skirmish settle in long streaks over the valley just beyond, while upon the hills, in long lines, were posted the rebels.

During the night, our whole corps by division, was moving up, with Carr and Osterhouse in the lead, and when they struck the rebel lines, this skirmish ensued; our forces thought it best to await the coming of the morning before further action. So at daylight, our forces were coming up and going into position, with Osterhouse on the right, Benton on the left, and Hovey in the center, while our division (A. J. Smith) was held in reserve. Firing commences on the right, then on the left, and then in the center, while our army is slowly advancing over hill and through cane-brake and under-brush; Benton's men make a charge, and the 18th boys are being cut up; now the 11th boys are falling, and all along the line the battle is raging, while we are being rushed from one point of the line to another; strengthening a weakened place here, and then moving at double quick to another; as they drop back and form another line upon one of the hills, our lines were pushing their way up through the storm of minie-balls and bomb-shell; as the battle ebbs in one place, it rages in another; but our lines are gaining hill after hill, and along in the evening our regiment is put in the front, and in line with others, makes the last charge. The rebels leave the field and we have won the victory.

The battle lasted all day, during which we suffered severely from thirst, and heat from the sun's scorching rays. There were captured 650 prisoners and two batteries; while the Union's loss was 130 killed and 718 wounded. As the sun sinks in the west, we, all worn-out and exhausted, with nothing to eat or drink since the evening before, drop down upon the blood-stained grass, among the dead and wounded, and pass the night.

The following morning, after partaking of our hard-tack and coffee, we found the rebels all gone, and we advanced toward Fort Gibson. Our army had gone but a short distance, when, under a flag of truce, a delegation of ladies came out to formally surrender the city. The mayor, having been wounded the night before, this duty devolved upon his wife, who had gathered a staff of ladies around her to assist in to perform this responsible duty; but before the advance guards were then in the city passing out as the rebels had started on the bridge across Bayou Pierre.

We remained here all day and night while this bridge was being repaired. On the morning of the 3d, we moved over the bridge and went in pursuit of the retreating rebels, marching all day over a somewhat broken country, until we came to a place called Willow Springs, where we found plenty of fresh water, and captured a few pork sheep, which on being dressed, looked thin and blue, but we tied them fast together and hung them on a pole over a fire, and soon we had roast mutton for supper, and being much in need of rest, we camped here for two days. On the 5th we resumed our march, over dry and hilly roads, in a northerly direction, until late in the evening, when we came to a place called Rocky Springs, on Five Mile Creek, where we stayed two days, while other portions of the army were moving on the roads. As our three day's rations (drawn at Bruinsburg) were exhausted when we left Port Gibson, we now had to live on what we could gather from the country about us, and as the rebel army was retreating before us, and we having a large army of our own, it became very difficult to procure sufficient supplies for our subsistence; but one who has never tried it cannot know how little a soldier can live on. On the morning of the 7th, we were again on the march, moved up some miles, and were thrown out as a rear-guard to the main army, and encamped in a little valley called Fourteen mile Creek. There was but little water and less to forage, and after spending the night there, on the morning of the 8th, we were drawn back to the main road, which, by this time, had become very dusty; and this day, we suffered from dust, thirst and heat, and as many other troops had preceeded us, we found but very little to subsist upon, while water was scarce and filthy. Late in the evening we arrived at Cayouga, where we found a beautiful grove to camp in, but there being no creeks or other running water in this vicinity, we had to resort to stagnant ponds for water, where we could rake away the green scum, and eagerly quench our thirst, and fill our canteens to make coffee for supper.

While here, late one evening, all dusty and fagged out, came along the 8th Wisconsin regiment. As they were passing along, we observed upon one man's shoulder, a full-grown American eagle; but he seemed to be weary of his long, hot ride, as his mouth was open and his wings drooped; and his woe-begone appearance resembled anything else than the proud "American Eagle." On the morning of the 11th we left this place and moved on the Auburn road; going but a few miles, we halted, and having but little success in procuring anything to eat, we now began to suffer somewhat from hunger—one was peculiarly fortunate who could boast of more than one ear of corn and it was common to see a soldier holding on to his ear of corn as though it was the connecting link between life and death.

This corn we would parch and pound up, or grind, (if anyone was fortunate enough to be in possession of a handmill) and then make it into a cake and bake in skillets or roast it in the ashes. But while we were here, our teams came up, bringing our knapsacks, which we had left at Bruinsburg on the 30th of April, and also a supply of hard bread, which was gladly received.

On the 12th we moved in the direction of Raymond, but only going a few miles when we halted. We knew the enemy was not far off; and it was on this day that Logan met and defeated the enemy at Raymond, with a loss of 440, while the enemy's loss was 450 killed and wounded and 415 prisoners.

On the 13th we moved up in the vicinity of Raymond and encamped near a little creek, where we captured a few hogs, which, with our hard bread, made a fine supper. After passing the night here on the morning of the 14th we crossed this little creek and marched in the direction of Edward's Station: going but a few miles, we halted, putting out a heavy skirmish line, and in line of battle, lay here all the evening. During the night a heavy rain and thunder-storm came, drenching us to the skin; and the following day we remained in line of battle, ready for action and advancing but little.

Now, when we (the 13th army corps) left Milikens-Bend on April 1st, we left the 15th corps there, and when we were about to make an attack upon Grand Gulf, Sherman with the 15th corps, was making a feint upon Haynes Bluff, to divert the attention and draw the forces of the enemy from us, but as soon as the battle at Port Gibson had been fought, then Sherman withdrew from Haynes Bluff, and by forced marches came down on the Louisiana side, and crossed the river at Grand Gulf and came on, passing us near Cayuga, and went on and fought the battle of Raymond on the 12th, and hurried on after Johnson at Jackson. Miss. While we during the last few days were making short marches, and now lying in line of battle here watching the enemy. Sherman had gone to Jackson and driven Johnson away; while Pemberton, the rebel general, had been drawing all his forces that could be spared from the works at Vicksburg, and placing them in position to make a determined stand on Baker's Creek, just in our front; and all day, on the 15th, while we are lying here in line of battle, Sherman's men, by a forced march, are coming to join us on the extreme right. And on the morning of the 16th, while Hovey was moving his division into line, it blocks up the road and impedes Logan some hours, and before Logan had gotten into position, the rebel hosts were contending for Hovey's position on Champion Hill, and this hill being the key of the situation, with great fury the battle opened upon Hovey and Logan; while it was not so heavy on us, the brunt of the battle was falling upon Hovey. We kept up skirmishing and fighting during the day, and when evening came, and the sun, like a great red ball, set beneath the heavy clouds of smoke and drew a veil of darkness about us, and the moon refused to shine; while the Gods in the heavens, through the twinkling stars, refuse to look upon this field of carnage, and the soft breezes of the dark, still night, bear to our ears the groans of the dying; while here and there, groping among the wounded and dead, were men hunting out their fallen comrades.

We lay here during the night, and when the light of the morning of the 17th came it revealed the field clear, and the rebels gone, and after a hasty breakfast we soon were on the road in pursuit, and with skirmishers in front, and on both sides, we moved briskly on the Black River road, over broken roads, and amid the cast-away armor of the fleeing enemy.

We were not long in coming up to the breaks of the river, where we could see the broad grassy valley stretched out before us, and upon the farther edge of which we could see heavy breast-works and rifle pits, and upon the opposite hills were the hosts of the rebel army, determined to make a stand; and now one of the most beautiful pictures of war presents it self.

Upon this beautiful Sunday morning, the light of the great golden Sun was fringing the forest and hill in rolls of golden beauty, while we in long lines of blue with waving colors and glittering armor, lay there over-looking the grassy valley below, while on the opposite hills might be seen great glistening cannon and a great host of rebel colors were fluttering in the breezes, while at the foot of the hill, at their feet, ran the river, upon whose banks bristling cannon lay charged with messengers of death.

We had halted to await support and get into proper place to make a charge across the valley, when suddenly we heard a yell, which was taken up and passed from brigade to brigade along the whole line, and instantly without orders, started upon a charge, when a storm of shot and shell from the rebel batteries was screeching and howling about us; our batteries responded, hurling solid shot and shell into the ranks of the enemy. While on a run the lines in blue pushed forward up near the enemy; they are now in rifle shot, and the deadly minie balls are peltering like heavy rain-drops, and we fall flat upon the ground to catch our breath, while the storm of deadly missiles (from both ways) pass over us, then up! and with mighty yells, on, on we go, when the white flag comes, and we (our regiment) capture more prisoners than it has men.

The rebels had set fire to the R. R. bridge and it was now burning so as to prevent the enemy themselves from crossing, and many jumped into the river and attempted to swim across, when we would halt them and make them swim back and become prisoners. In this battle our forces captured fifteen-hundred prisoners and eighteen cannon, and a great many small arms. While our loss was 271 killed and wounded. The bridge being destroyed, we were obliged to remain here until we could construct one, but on the morning of the 18th we were up and moving in pursuit, and never stopped to ease our breasts by panting, until we called both city and field ours.

With our skirmish line well in front we moved on at a rapid march, while the sun poured down its scorching rays and the dry ground reflected the heat, and the dust filled the air almost to suffocation, while the water was scarce and filthy. All combined to make this one among the hardest marches we had endured, and many, overcome by heat and fatigue, fell by the wayside worn out, foot-sore and famished, while the main body kept on until in the evening, when coming up within two miles of the rebel works at Vicksburg, we halted for the night and lay down on the green sward to rest from our hot and weary march; and during the night many of the boys who had fallen by the wayside during the day, now invigorated by the cool night breeze, came up, and after a night's rest here on the green grass, on the morning of the 19th we were up and soon in line. We had moved but a short distance when we came in sight of the rebel works in our front, and extending in long lines both to the right and to the left, and in the bright sunshine of the morning we could see the great forts studded with glistening cannon, while along the rifle pits and breastworks could be seen the rebel armies beneath their waving flags, awaiting our arrival. Just beyond these works and hills, glistening in the bright sunshine, were the spires of the city, the object of all our long marches and hard fighting. But between us and that goal lies miles of rebel works, manned and defended by 35,000 well trained and disciplined soldiers, determined to contest our right to that city, even unto the doors of death.

Now Grant, availing himself of the demoralized condition of the rebel forces, had ordered an assault upon the rebel works as soon as our lines could be placed in position about the works. So Sherman upon the right; McPherson in the center and McClenard on the left, all had their men in position and in long lines, broken only by the ruggedness of the ground. Thus lay the army in the broiling sunshine, tired and worn out from their long marching and fighting, all ragged and powder burned; and now while awaiting the order to charge great drops of perspiration coursed down their faces, when, suddenly the signal is sounded and they spring out with a mighty yell, push their way down ravines up declivities, and across gullies some times in single file and some times in double, while a hail storm of shot, shells and minie balls fill the air about them as they push from this point to that, running the gauntlet of death.

All the evening this firing was kept up, but when it was found that the works could not be taken before the evening sun should set, we ceased firing, and the night's dark stillness settled down upon both armies; and we had failed to take the place. Grant then ordered us to positions of safety from the enemies fire, and a much needed rest.

We had marched nearly 200 miles; fought five battles and had lived upon the three days rations drawn at Brünsburg, eighteen days ago. Now, Sherman, in our rapid march upon Vicksburg, had flanked the enemy out of the works at Haynes Bluff, and established a base of supplies on the Yazoo, and while we were making this last assault, great trains of wagons filled with rations were coming as fast as they could be driven, and while the sun goes down, the teams come up, and we again draw rations, soap and clothing; pools of water and springs are sought out, fires in the deep ravines are made and coffee is boiled; we once more had a supply of coffee, hard-tack and bacon; then all except the pickets drop down and sleep; that sleep which only the worn out soldier can appreciate.

On the 20th and 21st the order of the day seemed to be bathing, dressing and resting, while our artillery was being brought up and batteries were placed in position as near the enemy as possible, while the space between us and the rebel works were scanned through field glasses, by the commanding generals, preparatory for a grand charge on the 22nd.

This charge was to take place at 10 o'clock, and we were to take nothing with us but our arms and accoutrements, one day's rations and our canteens well filled, and every piece of artillery along the whole line should open fire early in the morning and continue until the hour of ten should arrive, when all should cease.

Early on this morning (22nd of May,) the batteries all along the line opened their sulphurous threats and vomited a torrent of shot and shell upon the rebel minions, while Porter over on the river front was pouring upon the doomed city, a heavy storm of iron hail, and for five hours, thirty batteries upon the land and Porter's fleet upon the river, kept pouring in a storm of death upon the city and the rebel works; filling the very vaults of Heaven with sulphurous smoke, while the sunshine turned the hills about us to the color of blood. The Heavens trembled and the earth shook, while this heavy cannonading continued. Meanwhile, our boys were filling up their canteens and buckling on their arms, and the skirmish line and sharp shooters were working their way well up to the forts, while the main line lay awaiting the signal of that awful moment.

When a few minutes before ten all the batteries cease and Porters's fleet has stopped firing, and a silence fell upon the army, and with blanched cheeks and determined brow; awaited the signal, while

> "Heaven and Earth are gazing upon us;
> God begirt with his power;
> We crowd the hope of centuries,
> Into this passing hour."

Every experienced soldier knew what this calm portended, and with every nerve strung up to high tension, awaited the signal to do or die. When along the lines the signal came, and in a moment with flags in front, the troops spring forward, readering the air with yells and clinching their guns as they start upon the charge; but in a moment the whole rebel works and rifle pits were one blaze of fire, while twenty thousand muskets and one hundred and fifty cannon belch forth death and destruction into our advancing lines, and great columns of smoke rose up, and as it were, turned the scorching sun into a great ball of blood, while a great halo of red light settled upon the hills, while the shot and shell, grape and canisters threw up great clouds of dust, hiding our columns from view, while the air was filled with suffocating smoke, through which, screaming shells, whistling balls and zipping bullets ploughed their way into our ranks which are slowly working up this ravine and across that ridge, running the gauntlet of death. Our ranks are now becoming decimated, and McClenard calls for support.

The 59th Ind. boys come around to our support, but the rebels have seen this part of their line hard pressed and they have reinforced, and now the hills that our columns have just passed over is but a field of death, over which none could pass and live, while our boys are seeking protection behind knolls, and many in the ditch beneath the rebel fire; while the 59th boys are picking off heads that dare rise above the works, and it is certain death to advance or retreat.

Now the lines are falling back, all along the line, and this charge is a bloody failure; and those in the ditch are left, and while the hours slowly pass away they watch for the going down of the sun, that they may, in the shades of darkness, make their escape; and the hour arrives and, one by one, they crawl out and sneak their way through pools of blood, over the dead, and among the wounded; and finally reach the lines.

The whole line had retreated, and left its dead and wounded upon the field where they fell, and now the curtains of darkness are spread, like a pall of mourning, over the terrible scene of the dead and dying; and as the darkness closed in, God, in his all-wise provision, sends a drenching rain, that quenches the thirst of the wounded, and cools the brow of the dying.

This was one of the grandest charges of the war, in which Grant loses a tenth of his command, and the 67th lose forty-two. Early next morning, a flag of truce was sent in, asking to care for our wounded and bury our dead; but this was refused, and our wounded and dead remain upon the field, while the army settles down to a regular siege. Pemberton, on being cooped up in the city, found that he had many surplus mules and horses consuming his supplies, and he immediately turned them out between the lines and our boys shoot them down; and the hot weather and sunshine, in a few hours, putrifies them; and, in connection with our dead, raises such a stench in the air that on Sunday they were glad to accept a flag of truce to bury the dead; and our boys who had lain there since Friday were so putrified that we could not move them, but roll them in a ditch dug by their side; while vermin were working in the wounds of our wounded

Now a regular siege had been entered upon: engineers were laying out lines of ditches and trenches, and picks and spades are brought up, and digging ditches, rifle pits, and tunnelling was the order of the day; and while sharp-shooters were keeping the rebels down and picking off their artillerymen, protecting us while we dug, and made tunnels towards the rebel forts.

Each day found us nearer than the preceding one as we advanced our picket line and constructed new ditches each night, while at no time, day or night, did the firing on either side cease during the siege, and from day to day, and week to week, in the broiling sunshine by day, and in the darkness of the hour by night, this firing, digging and tunnelling continued, while heavy batteries were brought up and placed in position along the whole line, until there were one hundred and sixty heavy pieces in position on our side, and one hundred and fifty on the rebel side; and it became a practice on our side, at 10 o'clock each day, to turn all these dogs of war loose upon the enemy for an hour or so. During this time, the rebels sought their bomb proof, and remained silent.

In due time some of our ditches reached the rebel forts, and a tunnel was dug beneath them, and a mine of tons of powder was placed beneath; and one of these mines being in readiness, over in Logan's front, and an hour set to touch it off; and as the hour approached all eyes were turned in that direction, when suddenly there was a great upheaval, a heavy puff of dust and smoke, and the earth trembled, and a terrible concussion rent the air. But this did but little damage, except to create an uneasiness in the rebel forts, lest others might be blown up at any time.

Without much variation, the siege progressed slowly, until the 30th of July, when Pemberton sends over a flag of truce, asking conditions of surrender, and on learning unconditional surrender were the only terms the bearers of the message return; but in the evening Pemberton himself came over, and after some parleying agreed to surrender at 10 o'clock on the next day, the 4th of July. This glad news spread like wildfire all through the army, and when the morning of the 4th came, with eager expectation all came up to the front to witness the surrender, and when the hour drew near all were impatiently looking for the white flag to appear; when, in a few hours, it fluttered in our front, and in a few minutes, away to the right and left, one by one the white flags were placed upon their forts, and then long lines of blue, with stars and stripes fluttering, appeared upon open ground, and gave three of the longest and loudest cheers that any Fourth of July ever witnessed; then the rebels, by regiments, marched out in front and stacked their arms, and returned inside their works prisoners of war. Thirty-two thousand prisoners, one hundred and fifty cannon, and thirty-five thousand stand of small arms were the trophies of the day.

No sooner was this accomplished, when we received orders to prepare three days' rations, and be ready to march early the next morning. After all our long marches and hard fighting and suffering, we were not permitted to enter the gates of the coveted city, but must resume our hot and long marching and drive Johnson from the state. On the morning of the 5th we were upon the march early, and marching over dry and dusty roads, beneath the hot July sun, all covered with dust, and almost famished by thirst, we arrived at Black river, where we camped for the night; and when the morning came we were early on the march upon Champion Hill road, and as it was known that Johnson was in our front we moved slowly. As the sun rose higher the heat grew more intense and our canteens began to grow empty and we began to suffer from thirst. When we came up to the battle-field of Champion Hill, the carcasses of the dead horses and mules killed in the battle of May 16th, and the half buried dead of both armies, created an unbearable stench in the air, while vultures were feasting upon the carnage of battle.

We pushed on, leaving this horrible sight, horrible stench, and horrible memories to the vultures and varments, and as we passed on we found all the creeks dried up, leaving no water, except stagnant ponds, in which Johnson, in his retreat, had thrown dead animals to ruin water for us as we went in his pursuit. And when thirst compelled us, we would rake away the thick green scum and quench our thirst from these putrid waters and fill our canteens; and thus, from our own canteens, we drank poison and death.

On arriving near Bolton, late in the evening, we bivouaced upon an old corn-field, and lay down between the corn-rows to pass the night; but we had been there but a little while when the whole heavens became overcast by black clouds. Intense darkness set in, the lightnings flashed, the thunders rolled and the winds howled, bringing torrents of rain, which, lit up by the flashing lightning, looked like silvered flames of fire; while the water arose in the furrows, driving us upon the little ridges for rest and sleep, while fences were being torn down and thrown in piles, upon which to sleep; and by the flashes of lightning one could see, here and there, a soldier (like a muskrat) crawl up out of the water and coil up on a ridge and replace himself, while in another part of the camp could be heard grumblings and mutterings, while off in another direction we could hear one crying out, "Knee-deep, and still rising!"

Finally, the storm subsided and quiet reigned for a while. In about an hour another storm came, and the scenes of the former were repeated; but the night wore away, and we had secured but little rest. The morning came bright, and the sun shining in all his glory; and, in our wet clothes, we were early on the move, and marched up near Clinton, where we came up with the rebel rear, and the cavalry has been skirmishing; but we move on some distance beyond Clinton, and in line of battle spend the night; and in the morning there was skirmishing in front; and in line of battle we move up little by little all day, and continue in this way up to the 14th, where we find ourselves near Jackson, and we throw up defences, while we skirmish with the enemy, while around to our right some heavy fighting is going on. But Sherman, finding the works much stronger than they were the previous May, determined not to charge them, but institute a siege, and was fast drawing his army about the city on both flanks, and on the 15th bombarded the enemy heavily, and had some hard fighting in places about the line; but on the morning of the 16th we found that Johnson had evacuated during the night, leaving the city in our possession, and we immediately set about destroying all public property, railroads, and anything that would be of service to the enemy; and this being done, we, on the 21st, started on our return to Vicksburg, and through another scorching day's sun, over dusty and hot roads, we marched to Mississippi Springs, where we camped over night, and early on the morning of the 22d we were on the march through heat and dust by those stagnant ponds and Champion Hill battle-ground, and reached Black river late in the evening, having marched 25 miles, and camped where we could get plenty of water to drink and bathe our blistered feet, and resumed the march early next morning. We marched back to Vicksburg and went into camp upon the beautiful bottom just below the city.

And thus ends the memorable campaign. Since the 20th of December we had been constantly on the move, not stopping for rain or flood, cold or heat, sickness or defeat; making one expedition in Louisiana and three up the Mississippi; have marched 250 miles, fought eight battles, and been under fire sixty-one days. And now we lay ourselves down upon this grassy sward and take a rest we so much need. With

"The hopes and fears, the blood and tears
That marked the bitter strife,
Are all now crowned by victory,
That gave the nation life."

CHAPTER IV.

NEW ORLEANS—BAYOU TECHE CAMPAIGN.

"To the Hero, when his Sword
Has won the battle for the free,
Death's voice sounds like a prophet word;
And in its hollow tones are heard
The thanks of millions yet to be."

We lay in this beautiful camp nearly a month, during which results of our terrible exposure during the last nine months now began to develop, in the form of typhoid and malaria fevers, rheumatism, and all kinds of diseases in various forms, and many, on this account, were furloughed home, some of which never reached their homes, but were mustered into the grand army above.

We drew new clothes and received two months' pay and had plenty of rations and time to cook them, and by a liberal use of soap and Mississippi water we once more got clean and felt like men again, and the health of the regiment began to improve while we were taking rest and recreation from active warfare. Meanwhile many of the invalids who had been furloughed home and sent to the various hospitals during the winter and spring, were now returning, and all was going on smoothly, without excitement or anything of any particular interest occurring until August 15th, when we had a detail of two men from each company working by relief alternately with a detail from a colored regiment loading ammunition in the hull of a steamboat. And when our boys just finished their relief, and were sitting upon the guards of the boat resting, and while the colored boys are working, a colored soldier drops a percussion shell, cap downwards, and it explodes, sending a piece through the boiler, exploding it.

and instantly timbers, boys and all were promiscuously flying through the air, our boys coming off with only some cuts and bruises, while the colored boys never more were heard from.

About this time our 13th army corps were transferred from the Army of the Tennessee and ordered to report to Gen. Banks, at New Orleans, for duty, and from this time on to the end of the war we serve in the Army of the Gulf. And after our month's rest and recuperation we, on the 24th of August, boarded a steamer, and, after giving three long cheers for the Union, shove off and move down stream; and as the warm August evening faded into a beautiful twilight, and a calmness settled upon hill and valley, it was pleasant to be upon hurricane deck, where we could enjoy the scenery upon the banks of the mighty stream as we passed down.

The hot August sun sunk below the western forest, and the veils of darkness had now set in, while the cool, damp breezes were arising from river and valley. It was delightful to set and enjoy the passing hours in silent meditation; when suddenly this happy silence was broken by sweet strains of music pouring from loyal souls upon the warm, soft breeze, which carried it from hill to hill and spread it upon the calm, silent valley. And as the evening had worn away we sought our ever faithful blankets and prepared to take our rest upon open deck, and our regiment was so few in number that we had no more need of "spoon drills," but there were vacant places by our sides for comrades who are sleeping, where

"No echo from this stormy past
Alarms the placid vale,
Nor cannon's roar, nor trumpet blast,
Nor shattered soldiers' wail;
There's nothing left to mark the strife,
The triumph or the pain.
Where nature to her general life
Takes back our lives again."

And, rolled in our blankets, we sleep while our boat puffs on her onward course as morning and evening come and go and we pass Port Hudson, Natchez, Baton Rouge and many large cotton plantations, 'till, on the 28th, we arrive in sight of the Crescent City, of which we had heard and read so much; and as we rounded the curve near the Old Red Church a beautiful picture presented itself of the city, hugged in by the lake and river; and as it now lays there, apparently asleep, gave no indication of its stormy past. As we neared the city the hurricane deck became crowded with anxious lookers. We were now near the city, and we round in and land at Carlton, some twelve miles above, and we are not permitted now to go down to the city, but go in camp on a beautiful grassy plain just below this little suburban village, and after we had well established ourselves in camp and had washed the dust and smoke from our faces and shaved—those who had beard to shave—and donned our dress suits, we went forth to take in the city, and here we found, built of huge stones, the great custom house, which, by its own weight, had sunken one story beneath the surface; then a little further on we find Jackson's statue, in all his rigid grandeur sitting upon his fiery steed; and then we come to the historic French Market, where we find all peoples, tongues and nationalities. In this market we can find anything that grows in tropical America.

But Gen. Banks was now organizing for a campaign, and we must forego the pleasures of the city and perform our military duty, and all was going on delightfully, when one day we received orders to pack up and go to Lake End (now East End) where we boarded a steamer, and, after loading on some teams and wagons, and all being ready, we shoved off and proceeded down Lake Ponchartrain, out by Fort Pike, and turned east through the waters of the Mississippi Sound, to what destination we knew not.

Now, we had a mule on board which was noted for his habit of pulling back, like some people, no difference at which end he was hitched, he wanted to pull the other way. When he was hitched to a wagon, when he was wanted to pull forward, he would set the other way, and when hitched by the halter he would soon try its strength by pulling back, so now we had him tied up by a heavy rope halter, and late this evening he thought to assume his independence by breaking loose; so he heaved and set; then, taking a powerful set, his halter broke and he fell back against the rail, breaking it, and head over heels he plunged into the depths below, and after going to unknown depths he finally took a reaction and came to the surface somewhat crestfallen, but he had a mule's ambition, and he struck out to explore the endless waters about him, and after swimming around a few times he spied an island in the dim distance, when he struck out for it; but as he swam it seemed to recede from him, and, becoming weaker, his heart began to fail him, and he turns for the boat and swims around it until he was about to yield up the ghost. All dejected, and with despair in his eyes, and his ears falling penitently, he comes up and surrenders, and we fasten ropes about him and pull him on board, a wiser and better mule.

We proceeded on our journey all night, and on the morning, near Mississippi City, we received orders to return without debarking, and we wheeled about and returned to our camp again, where, on account of our hard services during the past year, discipline was a little slack, and we enjoyed more liberties and leisure than ordinarily, and we need not say that these were improved to the utmost extent, and to say the city was well taken in would not express it.

And while we were doing the city, bathing in and boating on the lake, troops were coming in and going into camp near us, until this whole grassy plain became one canvas city; and now battallion drills, company and regimental inspection and grand reviews became the order of the day, these latter were laborious and exhausting, but such things must needs be in preparing for a campaign.

While we were undergoing all this a little transport on its way down the river was captured, its contents taken out, while she was burned somewhere opposite a place called

New River. So we were ordered to board a steamer to go up the river and chastise the rebels for this audacious act. So we steamed up to where the boat was burned, tied up and debarked and moved out across the broad bottoms and through cane-brakes so thick that they formed almost a perfect tunnel, without inlet or outlet, for miles, being the darkest and the gloomiest forest we had been in; but we finally got through to some plantations on a little bayou called New River. Here we found some of the captured coffee and rice, etc., stored away in some buildings, but no one to look after them, all having business elsewhere just then. We stopped here over night, during which a cotton gin filled with freshly ginned cotton took fire by spontaneous combustion. It seemed that our presence sometimes created *spontaneous combustion*. The flames from this gin ascended high up into the air, lighting up the whole country about, but no one came to help put it out, and it was burned to the ground. When the morning came, having found no rebels, we started to return to the boat, and had gone but a few miles when we found that by some means we had taken the wrong road; but a veritable tunnel as it was, we could not cut across the country to the right road, but had to retrace our steps or go forward. We chose the latter, and pushing forward we finally came out to the river some ten or twelve miles above the boat, and General Burbridge sent an orderly for the boat while we lay on the ground until the boat came, and thence boarded her and went to camp and resumed drill in inspections, etc.

The oasis in army life, like the great desert, are surrounded by the hardships of war, and so, with this, on the 8th day of October, we struck tents, and with the three days' rations moved across the river to Algiers, where we, late at night, took a train on the N. O. & W. railroad, and during the night were taken to Brazier City, now Morgan City, and on the same night crossed over Berwich Bay, some three miles wide, and went into camp near the great mounds, subsequently converted into a fort. Here we overtook the other divisions of the 13th army corps, and a part of the 19th corps, and while lying here a few days we had our first expericnce with fresh water soap used in salt water, as when we tried to wash our hands and face it acted like grease, and the more we rubbed the greasier we got, until the air became blue with the unwritten language of an irate soldier, and we knew no way out of this trouble until we learned that it required a different kind of soap for salt water.

In due time we struck tents and moved out and took the road up Bayou Teche and marched up as far as Pattersonville, where, on the edge of the bayou, we camped for the night, where, as the night closed in, great long-legged, bloodthirsty gallinippers made their appearance, and we had to skirmish and fight to save our very heart's blood; and as the dark, still hours passed by, we could hear in the swamps near us the bellowing of alligators, like a herd of lost bulls.

We were glad to welcome the morning, as we preferred a hot day's march to fighting a fruitless fight with those gallinippers; so we we were early on the march upon a dusty road skirted by tall cypress tress, whose tops were solidly matted together with long gray Spanish moss, whose shade made an inviting spot to rest in, where we rested ten minutes each hour; but as other troops had preceded us, we were deprived of much fun, as they had killed most of the alligators near the road, and as we passed along we saw legions of dead alligators, but found few live ones for us to try our Enfield rifles upon. Evening found us just below Franklin, where we went into camp for the night, and early the next morning we were on the move, and on coming up near this nice little city we straightened up, dressed our files and put on the best of soldierly appearance; and with music in front, playing "Star Spangled Banner" and "Rally Round the Flag," we made a grand appearance, while the citizens looked on in apparent astonishment, and on going on but a few miles we went into camp on the edge of the bayou.

During this hot day's march an old yellow mare came in to do service in the cause of the Union, and by some singular coincidence an old cart was brought in. So the Company A boys determined to utilize this cart and mare at once. So on the following morning, when all were ready for the march, Old Yellow was hitched to a cart-load of knapsacks, and during the long, hot day's march, did good service in hauling many of the foot sore and given-out boys, and when night came Old Yellow had plenty of feed, though the general's horse fell short, and when we we went into camp near Theia, Old Yellow again rendered important service by hauling in loads of rails, beneath which often lay a rebel hog; but after a few days' march, while Old Yellow was hauling knapsacks and sore-footed boys, some one complained to the general that some had their knapsacks hauled, while others had to carry theirs; so an order came to turn Old Yellow over to the quartermaster's tent, and with ropes entangled Old Yellow's legs and threw her to the ground and turned her over toward the quartermaster who was, all this time, ignorant of the cause of all this, but Old Yellow was back hauling knapsacks and blistered feet, and no more complaints were heard, as Old Yellow had been "turned over," as ordered. We by this time had gotten well up into a beautiful timbered country, where there were beautiful plantations and residences and many orange orchards, but as the 19th army corps, and the greater part of ours, had preceded us, these orchards did us but little good.

While we lay in camp near Vermillionville, apparently for some days' stay, suddenly we heard the boom of a cannon away off in front; then another boom, quickly followed by others, and in a few minutes we had orders to pack up and be ready to march in fifteen minutes; and by that time we were ready and on the march through Vermillionville, and on toward Grand Cateau, and all through that hot prairie we kept moving 'till late in the evening. We came up to the 19th corps just beyond where the firing kept going on, and we moved on well up to the front and camped for the night where the firing had been, neither seeing nor hearing any rebels, but on the following morning were up and on the move through Grand Cateau and beyond a little ways, and when we halted for the time, and after remaining here but a few days, we again resumed the march, and passing through Opolusus, the oldest town in the State (the old and dilapidated houses did not deny its right of title) on we went to a place called Barr's Landing, where we went into camp and immediately set about gathering in corn and forage, as though a base of supplies were to be formed here, and for a few days we kept up this business. Meantime General Green, with his division of rebel soldiers, moved up to Opolusus cutting us entirely off from the main army without any apparent way of escape from capture, but during the 31st day of October a colored man came in and informed Gen. Burbrage that he could pilot our little army around over cow-paths, through brush and forest, to the main army. So on that evening we cooked our supper and bivouaced for the night as calmly as though we never heard of General Green and his rebel hosts.

But no sooner than the dark curtain of night had closed about us than we quietly struck tents and moved out, following our faithful colored guide through mud, brush, and dismal forest, making it dungeon dark; but we kept on all night, and when morning came we had left the rebels behind and had formed a junction with the main army, and during this 1st day of November we went in camp near Grand Cateau; and General Green, on finding his game had left Barr's Landing, now began to seek us out and found us now forming the rear guard for the main army, and on the 2d he commenced harrassing us, and we were now skirmishing with his troops all day over these grassy prairies, and at one time during this day, while we were out there in line with a colored regiment on our right, while bombshells and shot were coming pretty lively, these colored boys struck up the tune,

"Rally 'Round the Flag,', and keeping their lines dressed, and while their loyal thoughts poured forth the music, step by step, on exact time, they moved, for aught they knew, toward the jaws of death and thus in line with us moved up; but the rebels gave way and we had but a skirmish and the night came on and both armies retired into their respective lines, and the night passes as though nothing unusual had occurred; so used to warfare were we that to skirmish all day with the enemy was but an ordinary day's work, and we would return to our camp and sleep as sound as the farmer from his harvest field.

The morning of the 3d came with nothing unusual in appearance, and when the ordinary duties of the morning were gone through with, the paymaster came up and paid company A, and was now paying company F; and while our fresh pork, that we had captured from the rebels the day before, was lazily boiling, suddenly we heard the pickets firing off in front, and thinking we had another day's skirmishing on our hands we, without putting on our coats, buckled on our cartridge boxes and grabbed our faithful rifles, and were in ranks in a few minutes and moving out by flank to meet the enemy, while the paymaster flew to the main army, some four miles away.

Now we had four regiments of our brigade in line as follows: The 67th on the extreme left, the 60th Indiana next, then the 23d Wisconsin, then the 96th Ohio, the 83rd Ohio having been sent out that morning after forage. This line, commanded by Col. Owen, of the 60th Indiana, moved out about a mile and halted with our regiment, swung clear out upon the prairie, while the right of the line rested in a skirt of woods, and we had not been there but a few minutes when, away to our front, we could see General Green's whole division of rebel troops in line of battle. At this time General Burbrage sends an orderly to General Franklin—the commander of the expedition—for reinforcements and Franklin replies: "Hold the place at all hazards." Meantime Green's whole troop is coming steadily over the prairie, when Gen. Burbrage sends his aid, Capt. Friedley, to Col. Buhler, ordering him to fall back, which Buhler refuses to do. When Burbrage again sends Friedley, peremptorily ordering Buhler to fall back to the woods. But it is now too late, as Green's masses were upon us with a heavy cavalry force pushing between us and the main army, and entirely surrounding us when our artillery was pouring shot and shell, while the rebel batteries were pouring a heavy fire of shot and shell into us; and now we open our musketry upon the advancing columns, and they pour a storm of minnie into our ranks; and by this time the cavalry was charging us, upon flank and rear, and our artillery had fallen back and was pouring into the rebels and us a storm of canister, while the rebel batteries were pouring into us and their men a storm of canister, while the rebel batteries were pouring into us a storm of grape; while at this juncture both forces became all mixed, and a pandemonium of sticking with bayonets, clubbing of muskets and shooting with revolvers. Meanwhile a storm of grape and canister was pouring into this fighting mass both from front and rear, while a cloud of smoke is spread over the scene, and we are overpowered and taken prisoners; and as they march us to the rear fire two loads of canister into us, but fortunately this last volley did not strike any of us, and thus Green's 8,000 men overpowered our 1200 troops, and are marching us off prisoners of war, while our reinforcements are coming on double quick, but they are too late. As they march us off the rebels fall back and the fight is over.

BATTLE OF GRAND CATEAU.

CHAPTER V.

PRISON LIFE.

> There are hearts with hopes still beating
>   In each pleasant Northern home;
> Watching, waiting, for the loved ones
>   Who may never, never come.
>
> In prison drear we languish,
>   Meager, tattered, pale and gaunt;
> Growing weaker day by day,
>   With pinching cold and want.

On capturing us, for fear our main army would recapture us, they rushed us along at a lively gait all evening, until we arrived at Opolusus, just beyond which we were corralled upon the open prairie like a herd of Texas cattle, and when the sun withdrew his warm rays, and the cool November night came on, it found us upon this bleak prairie without shelter or blankets, and without anything to eat or drink; and last, but not least, the most of us were in our shirt sleeves, having left our coats in camp when going out to meet the enemy.

And now, when the cool evening began to close in, our situation was anything but inviting, while the prospects for the night were growing more gloomy, as we were now becoming uncomfortably chilly and surrounded by the rebel guards. We grouped ourselves together in little groups and lay ourselves down upon the cold grass—not to sleep, but to rest and think.

Since our capture, we had no chance to converse with or even speak to each other without being hurried up by the guards; but now, in our miserable condition, while we lay on the cold earth and gazed into the blue vaults of heaven. It was a pleasure to be left with our own thoughts while we, in undertones, reviewed the day's battle; while we talked of our wounded and probably dead comrades left upon the field; and then in our minds, upon the chariots of thought, we reviewed our past hard marches and many hard-fought battles, where we had left our comrades beneath the sod of Kentucky; in the swamps and bogs of Louisiana; and how sickness and death had invaded our camp at Young's point, and filled the levees with our fallen comrades; and then of those that fell and now sleep upon Vicksburg Heights. And so on up to now we have three hundred left. Two hundred are laying here prisoners of war, and what our fate should be is in the unrevealed future; but, inured to dangers and hardships, we were ready to meet whatever was in store for us, and now, wearied from the day's battle and hard march and the night's reflections, all stiff with chill, we nestled together and dropped into a tired sleep. When morning came, we were glad to welcome the warm sunshine. We were early put upon the march without anything to eat or drink since the morning before, and moved off at a lively gait for about ten miles, when on coming up to some hog wallows filled with water we were halted and were allowed to quench our thirst by this precious fluid. While here we had issued to us a little corn-meal, which we had no means of cooking, but to make it into a dough and roast it in the ashes. As soon as our cakes were done we moved off gnawing our ash cakes like starved children, and after traveling some miles we came to an old sugar-house, where we re-halted for the evening without any rations; but our practical Hoosier eyes were not long in discovering a lot of old damaged molasses, which we were permitted to put into kettles and boil down and make a lot of taffy and had one taffy-pulling; not as a matter of fun, but necessity.

On the following morning we were put upon the move early. The news had preceded us that a large number of full-grown Yankees were to be brought through there that day, and the people from the rural districts were assembled at Chaneville to see the great free show, and on arriving there we found all the porches and platforms crowded, while in the background, in little knots the colored population were to be seen, and as we marched up through the middle of the street all eyes were eagerly gazing at us, but upon their countenances seemed to be a look of disappointment; but what it was we were unable to learn, until some of the more bold said to us: "Why, we 'uns thought you 'uns had horns, but you 'uns look like we 'uns." This solved the mystery, and there were many jests and remarks made at the expense of the Confedsracy as we passed through that town an unwilling show. We moved on at a rapid march. In fact, these rebels thought to march us down by long, hard and fast marches, but it was of no use; we were of Burbrige's brigade, and we were used to such marches; and they said that we were the d—est set of Yankees that they had ever seen; and so, on and on we went, each successive day being but a repetition of the former, and nothing of any particular interest occurring until, away up in the country, we come to an old cotton and sugar tramway, upon which was an upright engine and some flat-cars, which we were ordered to board, and we gladly obeyed, as by this time our feet were becoming sore.

All being ready, we moved off about as fast as we could have walked, but we were in no hurry to reach Tyler, the place of our destination, as we then thought, but after riding some fourteen miles on this tramway we were stoped at a sugar-house near Alexandria, La., where we halted and were assigned the open shed and lot for quarters, while the rebels reserved the main buildings for themselves. We were kept here from day to day with our hopes and fears alternating as the rumors came first that we were going to march to Tyler, Texas, and then to be exchanged. Meanwhile we were drawing our small allowance of black bread and about a quarter of a pound of beef bone and all for a day's ration;

while we were allowed to use a rick of wood near by to cook with. But it was now near the last of November and the days were growing cold, while the nights were extremely uncomfortable. We were afraid to use this wood liberally lest soon we should be without any to either cook or warm by; hence, while the cooking was going on, we absorbed as much of the waste heat as possible, and then passing the night in cold and darkness.

In the sugar-house there was a store-room built of brick, and having but one door, in which was placed a guard, and we were not long in finding out that there was a quantity of sugar stowed there, and a plan was soon on foot to get some of that sugar. On investigation it was found that the only way to get it was to punch a hole through the brick wall and carry it out behind the guard's back. So a committee on argument was to engage the guard in a heated discussion, while a committee on the "hole" was to punch a hole through the wall and carry the sugar off. This argument grew very hot and a little dangerous, but by some soothing jest smoothed things over, and finally all this ceased and the sugar was hid in little holes under the ground and beneath some old rags; but the guard soon discovered this trick and he cried like a child, saying that he would surely be shot. We were sorry we had done this thing; but we never learned what was done with the guard for his negligence. Now, while we were, like hogs before an approaching storm, we kept gathering up material, as opportunity would permit, to make a comfortable place to rest and keep as warm as possible. getting a shuck now and then, a stalk and a little bunch of grass until some had accumulated a right snug little bed. Sergeant Anderson, of Company B, by some means had come in possession of an old barrel in which he had deposited his bedding, and had a right comfortable house compared to others. Now, in this sugar barrel he could stow away the most of his headquarters, and in order to protect his outposts when the cold nights drew on, he would place it near where the fire had been so as to utilize the smouldering heat. Now, we all envied sergeant Anderson (his house.) While we were being tossed about by the wintry blasts he was snugly housed up in his barrel; but at a late hour one dark night we heard an unearthly noise like some one in the very agony of despair, and on looking in that direction we saw Sergeant Anderson's barrel all ablaze and he coming out wrong end foremost, like an imp of fire from the furnace of hades; but having his presence of mind, he tipped the barrel up and turned out all his combustibles, and he had his house left. Then we had lightnings and blue blazes, in the language of an inferno.

One day it was told us a negro had stolen a horse from some one and they had caught him and were going to bring him up there on a wheat bin. They brought him up and stripped him, tied his hands and feet, and now they were ready to show us how they whipped negroes, and a great burly fellow with a heavy leather strap in his hand commenced plying it upon the bare back, raising great welks of flesh at every stroke, while the negro was begging for life. When they had whipped him enough they put him upon a horse and started him off at full speed, twice firing a pistol at his receding figure.

We had now been here some time and the rumors of our exchange had become stale, when some of us began to plan an escape, but few being in the secret at first, but the plot grew rapidly, and finally many were in it, and we had no doubt but that the whole camp would assist when the proper time came; so a day was set and an hour appointed when two especially detailed should be near each guard, while all the others should be ready, and at a given signal the two nearest the respective guards should knock each of them down snatch their guns and make each of them prisoners, then charge upon the battery. Make them prisoners and mount the weakest of our crew upon mules and start for Natchez. Miss., mount ourselves as we marched through. But by some means the rebels found out our plot and tripled the guards and brought another battery up, and our scheme fell through. About this time we were moved over the river to a place called Pineville, where we were assigned a large planked-in shed for quarters.

As the storm of winter was upon us, and as we could have no fire in this shed, it was impossible for us to live there, and the rebels permitted us to go, and bring in pine logs and make fires outside the shed; by these fires we made our quarters both day and night. While we were here the rebels captured two of the 26th Ind., who made their escape from the prison at Tyler, Texas, and had made their way as far as the Mississippi river when captured, and were placed in a camp with us.

Finally one morning to our joy we were ordered into line and told we were now going to the Union lines for exchange, and we were moved back across Red River, with some doubts in our minds as to the truth of this matter, but on turning eastward we became assured of the fact, and our hopes arose and the day seemed brighter and the night came on when we had only made about seventeen miles and stopped for the night at an old sugar house, where with the exception of a few turnips, we lay down tired, hungry and supperless, with but little sleep, we passed the night anxiously waiting for the time to start on the march which came at last, having no breakfast to prepare or toilet to arrange we were soon upon the road and nothing of interest occurring, we made several miles and again stopped at an old dilapidated sugar house where we received a small allowance of black corn bread which we were then in fine condition to appreciate and after voratiously consuming a portion of this bread we reserved a small portion to march upon the next day and now being weary we lay our emaciated forms upon the ground beneath the shed for rest and sleep and the night closed in dark and still, nothing was heard but the hooting of the night owl and the guards lonely tread.

Now, one of those 26th Ind. men spoken of on a previous page, was a ventriloquist, and availing himself of the superstition common in the south. this dark still night, he thought to have some fun by practicing his art upon the guards. After posting us upon the matter he called for an imagined Sam who answered from the dilapidated loft. He then inquired of Sam what his business was up there; Sam said he was getting out, (his voice indicating squeezing through a crack) and in a few moments, thump ! something appeared to fall upon the ground outside. The rebel guard ran around to catch Sam but Sam was gone. Soon another (Jim this time) squeezing out and thumped upon the ground and the guards ran in search but Jim had made his escape; now the rebels placed a guard up there to prevent any more escapes, but queer noises were heard in different parts of the old building which had now worked up their superstitious feelings to a high pitch, and the poor guard upon that old loft was trembling so as to make the old floor rattle, but finally all was still and the night passed off; but next morning we had to be counted several times but none were absent and the mystery remained unsolved as far as the guards were concerned. We were soon on the march, but soon began to rain one of those cold, marrow, chilling December rains, and continued to rain all day, while we, in our half nude and starved condition kept plodding our way over the miry roads, wading branches and sloughs; night came and found us near New Washington about ten miles west of Opolusus. here we turned off into a piece of wood and stopped for the night. Now we were chilled to the marrow by the December rain, in a woods where nothing could be found dry enough to make fires with; hungry and worn out, and in our nude condition must lie down upon the watery earth and pass the night, hovering about our little fire (attempts of fire) and consuming the last crumb of our black bread, and now exhausted we piled ourselves down beside a log or chunk, or a root of a tree; warming each other with what little warmth we had in us, we proceeded to pass the night. While the winter blasts continued its gusts of rain among the naked forest and naught was heard except the winds lonesome moans, broken now and then by the lonely hoot of the night owl. The rain-drops pattering upon the dead leaves about us beat the passing throbs of human life as that terrible night passed —and the morning came, when we crawled out of steaming beds of wet leaves; glad to warm ourselves by exercise by crawling out early. To our joy the great beautiful Sun sent his warm rays to our relief, and as we moved along our clothes became dry, and again we felt in comparative comfort, and this days march brought us up near Grand Cateau, where we stopped near the place where we were captured, and camped in the cypress forest from which we had tore the long gray moss, and for the first time since our capture we had comfortable warm beds.

On the morning of the 23rd of December, the Sun arose clear and bright, and on preparing for the days march, we found that through our terrible exposure, several of the boys were now unable to march and after many threats the Rebels procured a few ambulances in the shape of ox carts, and dumped the sick boys in, and again we were all on the move while the day grew warm. After marching a few hours we came up to Vermillionville where we were halted upon the outskirts where we all piled down upon the ground for a little rest. Suddenly there was a slight commotion in front and looking in that direction we saw on the main street, a delegation of ladies beneath the rebel flag marching up in column, and now our curiosity was excited to know what all this meant. On reaching the rebel commander, they opened a protest against the "*obnoxious stinking Yankees,*" passing through their town and our commander was not long in submitting to their protest and we were turned to the left and through mud and water from ankle to waist deep, we marched all evening. Some of the boys, poor, wet and emaciated staggered, plunged through this mud and water hour after hour, and becoming entirely exhausted fell by the way-side, when a guard would come up with a revolver in his hand, and threaten the prisoner with instant death if he did not get up and move along. When the prisoner would tell him if he thought there was any honor in shooting a helpless prisoner to fire away, he could not move another step when after some reluctance, they brought up the ox cart ambulance, and two of them would gather hold of the prisoner, and throw him in the cart like a dead hog. But finally we got through and dragged our way on to New Iberia where we went into camp upon the ground beneath an old shed and as the darkness of that cold December night closed in, we, all muddy, bedraggled, cold and exhausted, lay down upon the cold ground to pass our cold Christmas eve, and while the wintry blasts were playing a tune of solemn mourning among the Cypress boughs, and the death chilling hours were passing, the poor, pale emaciated soldier with the chill of death upon him, nestles closer to his comrade; his limbs are growing numb, while a shudder of chill passing through his body, he nestles still closer to his comrade, a sleep comes over him, and he dreams of his happy home; he is sitting by his fire side and his little ones are about his knee like cherubims of angelic beauty. His loving wife moves about him like a goddess of light and beauty. He sees great doors swinging open and beholds festive plenty, then a cold tremor passes through his stiffning frame, and his glazed eyes look up in to space and beholds the stars dancing while the moon swings around while an angel robes him in the drapery of heaven, and Peter Rogers, of the 60th Indiana, passes through the gates of eternity, and all is dark and still.

When the morning came, anxious to warm up our benumbed limbs, we were soon in line, when a spirit of sadness came over us to see the cold stiff body of our comrade lying there upon the cold ground asleep in death, after suffering and enduring the hardships of prison life, and living upon the hopes that in a few short hours he would be among friends, and almost in the sight of the goal of his hope, death steps in and closes his eyes forever and with sadness on our brow and tears in our eyes, we move off and leave him forever.

After marching some ten or twelve miles which seemed to be the longest miles we ever marched—we came up to the place of exchange. Oh, how beautiful looks the starspangled banner; what a thrill of joy passes through our souls as we come here where we, in a little while will be exchanged. As our forces had not enough rebel prisoners to exchange the remainder unexchanged were paroled. Then we received some good old hard tack and a hunk of boiled pickled pork and a dram of whisky and, notwithstanding all the temperance fanatics in the world this dram was in place. After remaining here 'till late after midnight we boarded a small steamer, and felt our way slowly and carfuliy down the bayou, as it had been rumored that a squad of rebels had gone around and placed torpedoes in the stream to blow us up after our exchange, but we passed on safely and arrived at Brazier City, where we took a train to Algiers and on the morning of the 31st of December we crossed over to New Orleans where by our escort we were formed in line and moved up and for some purpose we were halted on a street just below the French market and while remaining here, all ragged and dirty and pine smoked and having a rebel hat here and a jacket there and rebel pants now and then, presenting such an appearance that no hoosier mother would have recognized her own son, meanwhile rebel ladies were peeping out from behind their closed window blinds, mistook us for rebel prisoners in the hands of the enemy and many of them with their hearts full of sympathy for their rebel cause, came forth and brought all kinds of delicacies, such as cakes, pies and pickles, while we with the ever presence of mind, kept mum until we had our fill of those good things when we hurrahed for the Union, and struck up the tune, "Rally around the Flag Boys" when, if a cyclone had struck that street it would not have cleared it of those ladies any quicker.

We moved on down in the lower part of the city and were placed in a large cotton yard, having a large shed on one end while the other was an open court or piaza, all being enclosed by a high brick wall having great double iron doors.

On the following morning, January 1st, 1864—noted as that cold New Years' Day—we drew new clothes and blankets with a liberal supply of soap, and after a seige of rubbing and bathing and taxing the neighboring barbers to their utmost capacity, we regenerated ourselves again into white men and donned our new suits.

And now comes the time when the closest friends must part; when we must part with those friends who had come to us in time of distress, who had stuck to us through all our suffering who had kept us interested in our midnight loneliness, who had always lived up to the scratch; but now with our change of fortune we and the grayback must part. So one by one we march out and place our friends enshrouded in our old rags, upon a funeral pile and offered them upon the altar of the rebellion, a living sacrifice to the God of prisons, while the great flames filled the vaults of heaven with noxious odors that could be sniffed afar off.

Now for a long time before we were captured we had dispensed with that useless appendage to voluntary military camp life—the camp guard and like free Americans had the freedom of the camp anywhere inside the picket lines; and now, after having been under guard by the rebels so long it seemed like a reflection upon our character, to be placed in this brick wall with heavy iron doors to keep us from breaking out and annoying the dear citizens. It was but a little while, while the guard was faithfully watching these great iron doors until some of the boys picked a large hole through the brick wall one night and proceeded to enjoy liberty by taking in the city and making considerable racket. Next morning the Provost Marshal had masons to come and fasten up the hole, and strengthened his guard, but the following night another hole was put through the wall and the dear citizens were again disturbed in their sleep, and the Provost Marshall was full of blue language. He was informed that if he would take away his guards and throw those iron doors open and give us the liberty to go and come as we pleased, he would have no more trouble. He, acting on this suggestion, next morning took away his guards and threw the great iron doors open, and all trouble ceased.

We remained in this camp, enjoying many liberties and the absolute freedom of the city, without anything of interest occuring until about the middle of March, when the weather was growing warm, and the monotony of laying here idle began to create a restlessness in camp, and we were moved out to Lake End (now East End) and quartered in an old evacuated hotel, where we enjoyed bathing and fishing in the lake and plying our skiffs over its waters, while nothing of interest transpired until about June 4, when we received the glad news of our exchange, and immediately set about preparing to join our regiment at Baton Rouge. In a few days we were on our way up the river, and on June 10, we, with many glad greetings joined our friends and companions, who were just off of the disastrous Red River campaign.

CHAPTER VI.

MATAGORDA BAY—RED RIVER CAMPAIGN

> Behold, in awful march and dread array
> The long extended squadrons shape their way;
> Death, in approaching, terrible, imparts
> An anxious horror to the bravest hearts;
> Yet do their beating breasts demand the strife,
> And thirst of glory quells the love of life.

In chapter V., we followed the fortunes of the captured portion of the regiment through the various phases of prison life until their final union with the regiment at Baton Rouge and we now dropped back to the battle of Grand Coteau and take up the fragment that escaped capture.

On that evening—Nov. 3, 1863, after the main army had come up and driven the rebels from the battle field, we buried our dead and exchanged, under a flag of truce, our wounded, among which were Captain Hendricks, of Co. A., who soon died, and Captain Sims, of Co. I. Then we fell back some four miles and stopped on the banks of Bayou Carrion Crow, and it was a pitiful sight to see but thirty-six there to stack arms, making, with those who had lost their arms in the battle, about seventy men left, and since the rebels had burned up all our tents and camp equipage, we were left here upon this bleak prairie without blankets, tents or food, but the main army being here we were soon supplied and our little squad lay down that night upon the bleak prairie and discussed the probable fate of our captured comrades.

Remaining with the main army as a fragment of the 67th Indiana we were doing our share of camp and picket duty, and soon, by slow marches, fell back to New Iberia, while the enemy kept up a continual skirmish upon our flanks and rear, resulting a few days after our arrival here, in a right smart fight, after which all settled down into a quiet camp life.

While here, through the efforts of Chaplain Chitenton and other chaplains, a considerable religious sentiment sprung up, and fortunately there was an old sugar house near by which the boys soon converted into a church house in which rousing religious meetings were held almost nightly, and as religion and patriotism are so near akin, it was not unfrequent when a rousing sacred meeting was at its highest pitch that a tune would be switched off into an outburst of patriotism, when the very walls would tremble and the roof shake with the soul-stirring strains.

We now had but little duty to perform, and were allowed much liberty, and it was not surprising that the surrounding plantations contributed largely to our commissary department; and while enjoying this little rest, Colonel Emerson, who had been absent since his wound at Arkansas Post, came up bringing with him a new flag and state banner for the regiment; but words cannot express his feelings at finding his regiment of 1,000 brave youths now reduced to a little squad of seventy. We remained here till the 8th of December, when we broke camp and marched to Brazier City, where we boarded a train and went to Algiers, arriving there on the 14th, and remaining but a few days, when we boarded a steamer and headed down the river, and soon came to the mouth of the Mississippi, where for the first time we beheld the Gulf stretching out before us, the great watery expanse, like unlimited fields whose bosoms were worked up into great blue waves upon whose crest splashed the foamy surf.

We soon passed out at the southwest pass, and our ship was riding the great blue waves like a thing of life, and we had not been enjoying this novelty long when there seemed to be a kind of rebellious feeling in our stomachs, and we soon lost interest in the rolling waves and with a kind of woe-be gone countenance we seated ourselves near the guard rail where, at each lurch of the vessel we would pour out freely large contributions to the inhabitants of the deep.

But nothing serious came of this seasickness and in due time we landed at Point Cavalo, Tex., on December 31st, where we went into camp upon a narrow neck of land about one mile wide and sixty long, being entirely devoid of timber, which compelled us to resort to driftwood for fuel, which we had to haul some eight or ten miles; hence we used the strictest economy in the use of the wood by digging little pits in the sand and building little fires to cook by, while we, by natural process, absorbed the escaping heat. While we were in this condition a great Norther came in all its Texas fury, bringing with it the fierce cold wind which filled the air with flying dust and sand. This cold, penetrating wind being so unbearable that we retreated to our tents and rolled up in our blankets. But we had not long been thus rolled up when orders came to march immediately; and this was one of the trying times which tested the nerves of the strongest, to crawl out of our warm blankets into this death chilling wind: but we were soon out and upon the march up the point, and after traveling several hours the storm became so severe that we were compelled to halt and seek shelter among the sand hills and by digging holes in the sand and nestling down together we waited the abatement of the storm. The night passed away and the morning came, but the storm was still raging, and a picket or two of some other command were chilled to death. When the storm was over we found that we had marched up some eight or ten miles, and accomplished nothing but the capture of some few sheep and when we returned to camp we found all our tents blown flat down. We soon erected them and remained a few days, when again our division, accompanied by three gunboats, moved up the point, and after marching two days came up near a fort, where we halted our commander, upon a gunboat, proceeded up the bay and with his field glass saw that the enemy behind their breastworks and in the fort outnumbered our force five to one, and that it would be a fruitless sacrifice of life for us to attack them, so a return march was ordered. The marching over this sand was so hard that many of the boys became footsore and were taken up by the gunboats and soon all arrived back in camp, where on the 20th of January our exchanged boys came to us. We had little to do, while the religious spirit that came over the camp while on the Teche had not abated, but on the contrary had spread over the whole army and daily meetings and baptisms seemed to be the order of the day. At one of these meetings, while the beach was covered with the assembled throng, Chaplain Chittenden led down into the water and baptized sixty converts.

While here, on February 12, 1864, our assistant surgeon by order, made a report of the condition of the regiment to the Medical Director of the Department of the Gulf, from which we quote the following: "Up to date there have been 17 resignations, 28 killed in battle, 13 died from wounds, 187 died from sickness, 97 wounded, 3 missing, 10 desertions, 97 discharged from general hospitals and since going into camp at Indianapolis, Oct. 27, 1862, 398 have been sent to general hospitals, of which 78 have returned," and now deducting all these numbers, including the 200 now in prison, we have but 64 left of the 67th, who are now attached to, and doing duty with the 60th Indiana.

We remained here until February 22, when we struck tents and boarded the steamer St. Mary, and set sail for the Mississippi again, finding the gulf smooth this time. We made good time and arrived at Algiers on the 24th and remained there until next evening when we boarded a train of stock cars loaded with hay. During this trip to Brazier City, Major Sears, in lighting his pipe, dropped a match into the hay and a blaze sprung up. The only way to stop this blaze was to empty our canteens upon it. The first canteen emptied proved to be "commissary," which added fuel to the flames and we were upon the verge of a panic, when we finally quashthe flames and all went on smoothly. On arriving at Brazier City we debarked and crossed the bay and went into camp near two large mounds, which were converted into forts. After remaining in camp here several days, during which about 150 non-veterans of the 60th Indiana were attached to the 67th; and now with this number attached we were about 300 strong, and marched up to Franklin. While here the 19th Corps overtakes us and goes in front, and now we have two depleted brigades of the 13th Corps and the 19th Corps, all under command of Gen. Wm. B. Franklin, and as Colonel Emerson was the ranking Colonel, he takes command of the brigade.

On March 16th, with ten days rations, we set out upon the march up the Teche. Gen. Franklin seemed to be very severe upon us western troups and issued very severe orders against foraging, but nothing of any moment occurred until we reached a point near Vermilionville. Now it will be remembered that this is the town where the ladies of the town had met the prisoners of the 67th Indiana and 23rd Wisconsin on the 24th of December and caused them to march around their city through mud and water all that evening, and this fact must have been known to Gen. Franklin, who on nearing this point, issued strict orders against foraging and the destruction of property. But our boys, as well as the 23rd Wisconsin boys had a cause for revenge, and as a stimulant to this spirit they came across one of the rebel guards who had stood over us while in rebel prison, and it required some little caution to save this fellow's life. We had not been in camp but a little while when the whole prairie was lit up by a burning sugar house. Gen. Franklin immediately put our regiment and the 23rd Wisconsin under arrest until the offenders should be found and arrested, but it was a fruitless search for no prying committee ever found out the perpetrators, and after our regiment had lain under arrest some days, Franklin thought he would probably have use for these regiments soon and he released them from arrest and on we went up the Teche, and after twelve days marching we arrived at Alexandria on March 27th.

On the 28th we left Alexandria and we now found the enemy and skirmishing was kept up all day and when we lay down at night we kept ourselves in readiness for a fight at any moment, but we had no fight and on the morning resumed the march, when the skirmishing recommenced and was kept up all day, and on the 30th we arrived at Natchitoches, where we remained several days awaiting the arrival of the gunboats and transports in Red River.

After the arrival of the gunboats and transports, with a small squad of the 16th Indiana Mounted Infantry in front, we resumed the march, and on the evening of April 7th, we went into camp near Pleasant Hill. The cavalry advanced on the Mansfield road and we had scarcely bivouaced for the night when we were ordered into line, as it was reported that the cavalry had struck the enemy in force. We lay in line of battle until daylight on the morning of the 8th when our regiment with a section of artillery, were ordered forward in double quick time. On coming into a small clearing full of stumps we hastily formed into line of battle and moved forward, passing the 16th Indiana regiment, which was now being held at bay by the enemy in force in the woods just beyond, and now the ball opened pretty lively, but, by the aid of the artillery, after a sharp fight, the enemy were driven back while we lost some wounded. Captain Moore, of the 16th Indiana fell wounded about this time.

Now the road here was extremely narrow, while the thick woods on either side were full of underbrush matted together by long green briers, making it almost impossible to move in line of battle, while the enemy fell back and took advantage of the best positions, from which they would pour a volley into our skirmish line, then drop back to another position and await our coming. Thus we continued until noon, our regiment being all the time in advance. About this time the 77th Illinois came up and relieved us, while we fell back and became their support.

About this time also, Lieutenant Colonel Webbs (?) of the 77th Illinois—well knowt to us all as a very cheerful man —came up. But now when he led his regiment into position he wore an unaccountable grave and serious countenance which attracted the attention of all who saw him. He went a few rods to the right, where in a few minutes he fell pierced by a bullet.

We continued skirmishing and working our way through this terrible jungle until about three o'clock in the afternoon, when we emerged from this thicket into a large open space, probably one-fourth of a mile wide by a mile long. By this time our cavalry were advancing into the timber on the further edge, and our brigade had formed in line on this edge, and rested in place until about four o'clock, when we advanced to the west side of the field where our regiment took position on the right side of the road and in the rear of a fence along the edge of the timber, while Nim's battery was near the road on our left. This place was called Sabine Cross Roads, near Mansfield. While we were thus lying in line of battle two or three other batteries came up and took position at the edge of the timber in our rear. Meantime the wagon train was coming up and forming a corral in the open space behind us, while the second brigade was our support in the timber in the rear of the batteries.

Thus at 5 o'clock we were lying, awaiting the awful moment when the deathly silence would break into raging battle. We had but little time to wait, as in a few moments, in two long lines of battle, greatly over-lapping both of our flanks the enemy advanced upon us and under cover of the timber and thickly matted underbrush, they were upon us before the ball opened. Never before did we see a battery work harder, faster or more effectually than did Nim's battery at this moment—hurling grape and cannister, and mowing great swaths through the lines of the advancing enemy. But it was but a few moments when the enemy were crowding around both our flanks, and not over fifty paces from us. We were compelled to fall back across this field, while the enemy opened a heavy fire upon our retreating lines, and came on like a cyclone, capturing the battery and turning our own guns upon us. It seemed an act of providence that enabled us to escape across that field alive, though many did fall killed and wounded. Here John Z. Murphy, of Co. F fell, mortally wounded, and Colonel Emerson fell wounded and was soon captured, while the main line found a new position in the edge of the timber in the rear of the artillery, but the enemy, in two strong lines, came steadily on, while we hurled a storm of minnie balls among them and the artillery were knocking great gaps through their ranks at every discharge. They closed up the gaps and came on yelling like infuriated demons, and in a few minutes again flanked us upon both flanks, and when the line reached our artillery our whole line was pushed back. By this time we had reached our wagon train, blocking up the only road, and soon all was a pandemonium of confusion of wagons, mules and men, all in one mass of disorganized animation producing a panic. It became a surging mass, struggling to get back, while the enemy were upon us and pushing by our flanks, and it seemed that every fellow was for himself, and flinging away our guns and knapsacks in one confused mass, we pushed back some four miles where we met the 19th Corps in line of battle across the road and hastening forward on the double quick. It was but a few minutes after this surging mass passed through the lines of the 19th Corps before the enemy flushed with victory, came pell mell upon this line, which gave them a powerful withering volley. This checked the oncoming enemy, and now darkness set in and the firing ceased. During the long weary hours of that night the disorganized mass kept plodding their way through the general throng, and next morning found us at Pleasant Hill, where the remnant of our regiment was reformed by

PREPARING COFFEE.

Lieutenant Colonel Sears, who was then in command of the brigade, while the command of the regiment fell upon Captain Hall. We had not been reorganized long before the 16th Corps, with Gen. A. J. Smith in command, came up, and owing to our weakened condition we were held in reserve, while the 16th and 19th Corps fought the battle of Pleasant Hill on April 9. But the enemy came on in such numbers that the whole army was compelled to fall back, and that night we were kept moving all night long—being our third night without sleep, and we were now suffering agonies for want of sleep and rest. Many moved along that night automatically, being almost sound asleep, but just before daybreak on the 10th we were permitted to drop down in our tracks and sleep an hour or two while the cooks were sent ahead to prepare coffee by the roadside, that we might snatch it as we went along. When daylight came we were upon the move, and having come up to where our cooks had camp kettles filled with hot coffee setting upon stumps by the roadside, as we passed, each soldier dipped his cup in and passed on, gnawing his hardtack and sipping his coffee.

We soon reached Grand Ecore, all footsore and weary and exhausted for want of sleep and rest, and on the following morning we were joined by the main army. We threw up temporary breastworks, felled trees and made an abattis, and lay here several days expecting an attack from the enemy, who refrained from a direct attack, but kept skirmishing around on both flanks endeavoring to cut off our retreat. So fighting was going on on the outposts both night and day, but on April 20th we left this place on our retreat. We had gone but a little way when we emerged upon an open prairie where the enemy thought to entrap us by forming their forces all around this space, under cover of the timber, while we were compelled to march through the open prairie. We soon formed our lines with the cavalry in the rear and the artillery arranged at intervals, while we, (the infantry) formed in line with the batteries. It was a beautiful sight, on this bright lovely morning, to see these long lines, with guidons, banners and flags fluttering. At a given signal all moved at once, when this open space was filled with deadly missiles from the surrounding woods, but undaunted we moved along, firing, while our artillery hurled their double loads into the enemy. All advanced together, the batteries keeping in line with the infantry, pulling their pieces along as they fired, and thus cutting our way through the rebel lines and pushing on to the Cane river. We found that they had proceeded us and had possession of the ford upon our only line of retreat. Things began to look very gloomy, but about this time our regiment, with other troops, waded the river above the ford and came down in the rear of the enemy, and after a brief skirmish the rebels retreated and the ford was clear, when the whole army passed in safety on to Alexandria, where we remained a few weeks, while a dam was being constructed so as to enable our fleet to pass over the falls. While here the paymaster came up and paid us off twice inside of one week, and while here, notwithstanding all the hardships we had gone through and that the enemy were yet all about us and skirmishing and bomboarding were yet going on, we were not to be deprived of a little diversion; and as there were numbers of squirrels in the woods, the boys thought to catch them, and it was a common thing to see a soldier with a hatchet in his belt climbing the largest pine trees to the top to cut off a limb, when the poor squirrels, limb and all, would fall among a thousand soldiers, eagerly watching for the fun and scaring the poor animals almost to death.

Now the weather had become quite warm and the water became warm and filthy, and to add to this it was no uncommon sight to see dead horses and mules that had been killed in the battles above come floating down, and among these, frequently a rebel soldier who had been mustered out came floating down and passed on to make food for the scavengers of the south—the turkey buzzards.

We left Alexandria in the early part of May, and advanced slowly and very cautiously, since the rebels were upon all

CUTTING OUR WAY OUT.

CHAPTER VII.

MOBILE BAY CAMPAIGN.

> "Oh, who shared them ever shall forget
> The emotions of the spirit—rousing time,
> When breathless in the mart the couriers met,
> Early and late, at evening and at prime;
> When the loud cannon and the merry chime
> Hailed news on news, as field on field was won,
> When hope, long doubtful, soared at length sublime.

After the prisoners joined the regiment at Baton Rouge on the 12th as set forth in chapter V we remained here doing the regular curriculum of camp and post duty, until July 15, when we embarked for the army of the Potomac; as we understood, the 13th and 19th army corps having received orders to that effect. But on arriving at Algiers, on the 22d and awaiting ocean transportation, orders came holding back our portion of the 13th army corps and we now parted forever from the remainder of the 13th and 19th corps, as they set sail for the east under flying colors, and we went in camp to await further orders.

We having perfected Hardee's Casey's and Scott's tactics were, while here, drilled in the French bayonet drills and had arrived at a degree of perfection in this drill, when we (our brigade) received orders to embark for Mobile Bay, under command of Gen. Gorden Granger. So on the 29th we embarked, one-half of the regiment on a steamboat, while the other half were stowed on two barges with some artillery.

These steamboats and barges (carrying the whole army) were crowded to their utmost capacity and seemed to us not a very enviable condition to cross the treacherous waters of the Gulf of Mexico.

Two great cables were extended from the two barges bearing the right wing, of our Regiment and fastened to a steamer, and then a common steamer loaded to its utmost capacity, towing two barges, loaded to the waters edge, with the rest of the fleet, moves down the great Mississippi and out upon the great Gulf; as it were, tempting the god of storms and daring the surging waves.

To us who had never experienced the force of storms, nor the strength of waves, it seemed bold and reckless. But we steamed out upon the salt water through the south east pass of the delta and at once felt the strong buoyancy of the slowly rolling briny swell while the storms seemed to hold their wrath and the wind refused to blow while we have a very pleasant sail to Ship Island, reaching this place on Aug. 1st, and lay at anchor all day, during which we had a fine time, bathing in the blue briny deep, when along in the evening, we noticed a commotion on the steamer, all on board rushing to one side and those in the water making a rush to get out as soon as possible. We soon learned that a man who had dove into the depths below, from the hurricane deck and while in the act of rising to the surface, had his leg snapped off by a shark, but the man came to the surface and was rescued; this accident put a quietus to our further bathing and cast a gloom over the entire brigade, as one man killed or crippled by accident, creates as great sympathy than a half dozen killed in active battle, where such was expected and looked for.

We remained here, on our boats and barges at night, and early next morning we moved on, skirting the land away off to the left of us ten or twelve miles while we were sailing over smooth and placid waters and the sun was pouring down upon us his broiling rays of heat almost roasting us like a mass of sardines. About 4 o'clock on Aug. 2d we have insight of Dolphine Island, our point of destination, the boat and barges bearing the right wing coming in on the left of the island and the boat bearing the left wing skirted around in front.

Now this island was guarded on the left by Fort Powell, situated midway between the main land and the island, while on the right and front was Fort Gaines and all around the island by a shallow beach, so shallow that we could not land our boats and barges within less than one-half of a mile of shore, and the only way to land was to run our boats as near as possible, and then anchor, jump overboard and wade out, and in due time, with cartridge boxes and knapsacks strapped high upon our backs when one after another, plunge overboard and soon the water from shore to boat, was full of humanity, feeling our way to shore upon which the rebels held control, but soon a squad reaches shore, a skirmish line is formed and moves out a little ways.

Then the artillery is, piece by piece plunged overboard while the watching humanity grasps and pulls them through the waters to the shore; then comes the horses and they are made to jump off and wade out while the little lifeboats are being lowered and stowed full of amunition and pushed ashore.

This operation formed one of the grandest spectacles of the war. While it went on hour after hour until all are landed and it being now dark and all tired and wet, bivouaced for the night upon a narrow neck of sand but a few rods wide and while we munched our hardtack without coffee and stretched ourselves upon the sand for a bed and the sky formed a covering, the great briny billows roll up to us and then receed seemed to threaten us with the powers of the deep.

We had lain here but a little while when dark clouds began to loom in the west, lightnings began to flash, while the mutter of the distant thunder began to roll across the dark and turbid waters, while the wind began to push the swells nearer us. The clouds came swiftly on, the forked lightning lighting up the foaming waters while the mighty thunder seemed to loosen up the very foundation of the earth. Now the wind began driving one surging wave after another across this narrow neck of land almost sweeping everything before them, while we, like so many drowning rats kept moving down on the island nearer and nearer the enemy.

WADING ASHORE.

> "I have seen tempests where the scorching winds
> Have riv'd the knotty oaks, and I have seen
> The ambitious ocean swell, rage and foam,
> To be exalted with the threatening clouds,
> But never till to-night, never till now,
> Did I go through a tempest dropping fire."

During the time, the right wing of the regiment, was plunging into the deep and wading out while the storm was raging, the left, upon their boats were stemming the storm and waves. On the morning of August 3rd the sun rose and shone in his beautiful splendor, bright and warm, which was highly appreciated by us, as we were still wet from our plunge in the sea and the drenching we received from the storm the night before. After eating our breakfast of coffee and well-soaked hardtack and drying ourselves as best we could in the warm sunshine, and the left wing having come up and landed, we were prepared to push on further down the island in search of the enemy. The skirmish line was advanced and we formed in column and moved out, cautiously feeling our way toward the fort till late in the evening when we struck the enemy's pickets and exchanged a few rounds, then we were halted and strengthening the skirmish line and making the proper disposition of troops and artillery all then bivouaced for the night.

We were just out of range of the enemy's cannon and in a thick pine woods, where we could make fires, boil coffee and broil our meat on sticks over the pine fire, the smoke adding a peculiar flavor to the same. While this was going on we opened up our wardrobes and hung our blankets about the fire to dry out the dampness still remaining, from the soaking of the night before.

After supper our pickets were advanced and drove those of the enemy back, while the main body of the troops moved up in line of battle and the attacked arms, took up spades—not the jack or ace of spades, but the real old dirt digging, life preserving spades that we use when sieging the enemy and by reliefs dug rifle pits and when the morning dawned we found ourselves near enough for our batteries to play upon the fort. And at the dawn of the morning sharpshooting began all along the line; and the seige of Fort Gaines was fairly inaugurated. This seige was nothing new to us who had been through the seige of Vicksburg—each soldier was a practical engineer and but few mistakes were made as to safety or in effectiveness.

We kept advancing the picket line, then the line of battle, digging new rifle-pits at each stop until we arrived within rifle shot of the fort where we could pick the men off the fort and from their cannon, until it became extremely unhealthy for a man to show his head above the works on either side. This order of things was kept up till the evening of the 5th, when after a severe bombardment from the fleet and land batteries we made a charge upon the fort and, in a few minutes time, it capitulated with all its garrison, cannon, a large quantity of small arms, ammunition and general supplies, our loss being one man killed and a small number wounded; the man killed was a member of the 34th Iowa who, in a spirit of daring got out into open view and dared the enemy to shoot him which they did, and killed him on the spot. The reason of our small loss was due to the comparative surprise we gave them, by landing and coming up from a direction in which the Confederate authorities had declared an impossibility, but we did, and proved that there was no such a word as "failure" recognized among such seige veterans as we were.

On the 6th of August took place one of the grandest and most brilliant naval engagements the world has ever beheld. The sky was clear and bright, the bay as smooth as a sheet of ice.

Off on the waters of the gulf could be seen, like so many hugh sea birds floating at will, eighteen ships of war (fourteen wooden men of war and four iron clad monitors,) and just inside the bay, under the protection of the guns of Fort Morgan, lay three rebel gunboats and the old ram Tennessee.

To reach these the Union fleet had to pass within a few

rods and directly under the heavy guns of Fort Morgan. The City of Hartford was the flag ship of the Union fleet, up in the rigging of which, lashed to the center mast was the gallant Farragut with glass in hand, and just beneath him on a platform, rigged up for the purpose was a battery of small field pieces. At 7 o'clock a. m., the fleet, in battle array, moved up two and two, side by side, and on arriving opposite the great guns of the fort the earth rending artillery thunder roars, the waves flap their wrathy foam and the earth and the sea tremble as if convulsed by an earthquake, while above the vessels great volumes of sulphurous smoke fill the air and hovers about the fleet so thickly as to hide it from view, except the bright flashes of the firing guns. A breeze sprang up and rolled the great curtain of fire and smoke aside and we could see our vessels pushing by the fort, while Farragut's field pieces poured the iron hail down upon the gunners in the fort like vengeance from the clear vaults of heaven, when, suddenly we felt an awful jar, the earth seemed to rock, the angry waves of the sea seemed to splash and pile up in heaps and the whole firmament of heaven seemed filled with a deadening and appalling roar—one of our boats had struck a torpedo which exploded carrying death and destruction to nearly all on board, having exploded the magazine and boiler, the ship going immediately to the bottom.

We saw some of the ill fated crew splashing around in the water while the rebel batteries were playing upon them with grape and canister, and amid a storm of deadly missles, a life boat from our fleet went to their rescue and succeeded in saving a few of them. While all this was going on our fleet had engaged with the rebel ram and other boats of the rebel fleet, and Farragut signaled for the fleet to close in upon the rebel ram Tennesee; then came such a plunging, splashing, flashing and pounding as the world has seldom if ever witnessed, lashing the waters into an angry rage and filling the air with great columns of black smoke and earthquake rumblings. From the midst of the smoke we could see flash after flash from the mighty guns, and could hear the poor sailors give cheer after cheer. At last a breeze came and rolled away the mighty sulphurous curtain, the awful roaring ceased and we heard cheer after cheer from our fleet and saw all but one of the rebel fleet led off as prizes. Mobile Bay was ours. Thus ended one of the grandest naval fights on record.

After this great naval fight, under the guidance of Admiral Farragut, on the 9th day of August, in the face of the enemy and just out of his reach, we crossed the bay and landed two miles above Fort Morgan, put out a skirmish line and formed a line of battle from the bay to the gulf, across the narrow neck of sand upon, which the fort was situated, then moved cautiously toward the enemy. This narrow neck of land is composed of sand hills as white as snow, and at this time of year was hot enough to roast an egg.

Upon these little sand hills were small shrubs affording us a partial protection from the enemies guns.

Over this hot field of sand and through these shrubs we felt our way, followed closely by our field batteries until we reached a point from where we could see the great glittering guns of the enemy bearing down upon us in ominous silence. Here we halted, stacked arms and took up spades and prepared for a seige. Digging picket holes and rifle pits was the order of the day.

No sooner was this done than the enemy let loose his great guns upon us, hurling hundred pound shells shrieking over our heads, raking and tearing up the sand we had just passed over, but it was now too late, for we were going down in the sand like gophers. We followed the same practice we did at Fort Gaines, by advancing little by little each night and protected by the darkness, dug our picket holes and rifle pits and planted battery after battery, while sharp shooting was continually going on all along the line. The 21st heavy artillery now came up with their heavy motars which we assisted to place in position, and on refering to my notes I find we placed one at an angle of 55 degrees, which by military men is considered very steep. This motar would send a fifteen inch shell two miles high and drop it upon the heads of the enemy in the fort.

During the seige, to protect ourselves from the enemies' shells and balls, we constructed bomb proofs over portions of our main line. These bomb proofs were constructed out of anything we could procure, such as old posts and slabs, brought up from the rear and placed overhead and covered over with sand deep enough to retard and check bomb shells and solid shot. In the midst of heavy bombardments shaking the very foundations of the earth, these bomb proofs were liable to cave in and smother and sufficate all beneath. One day we heard an unusual noise to our left, on looking in that direction, we saw that the bomb proof over Capt. Friedley's Co. I., had gone down, covering him and most of his company beneath the sand. Lieutenant Colonel Sears cried out, "There's another company gone to hell."

No order was necessary for us, but we rushed there, and amidst a heavy bombardment of screeching and bursting shells we scratched them out like so many moles.

The seige was being pushed day and night, and in the meantime we were making the best of our surroundings. We captured a very long seine and frequently a hundred or more would take it and go in the bay, right under the great guns of the fort, but so close that they could not be depressed to bear upon us. Here we seined fish by the wagon load while the rebels in their wrath would fill the air above our heads with screaming shells which striking the water beyond us would go skipping away on the waters, to each of which we replied with tantalizing yells. Just above us and in an arm of the bay, was an oyster bed, upon which, we drew frequently. It was a valuable auxiliary to our commissary department. One day while a squad of our boys were in front, behind hills, watching the enemy and trying to pick off their gunners, a hundred pound shell struck in the sand hill bursting and completely covering nearly all of them beneath the sand. John

Nunnally, of Co. A., escaping, grabbed the cleanest gun and retreated to camp. On being asked the trouble, he replied that "the other boys had gone to hell and he thought he would come to camp." We returned with him to the spot of the explosion, but found that the other boys had wiggled out and were ready for duty.

We said this sand was white and hot, its effect upon many of the men was so serious that a number lost their sight for a time, some becoming permanently injured, while the hot air and poisonous sand produced ulcers upon our feet, some of which never got well. On this narrow strip of sand we had no water and were compelled to dig holes near the bay and let the briny water filter through, it was extremely warm and filthy and full of malaria, to which many of the boys fell victims.

The seige progressed finely; and each morning found us nearer the enemy than the previous one. We soon got within rifle shot of the enemy and a continual duel was kept up day and night under a continual roar of artillery. On the morning of the 23rd of August all the mortars and batteries were ready, and the fleet under Admiral Farragut, in position on the gulf and bay some two miles away. The monitors lay in the bay near our extreme right. All was still and silent. There was no premonitory signs of an impending engagement. Suddenly a signal from the City of Hartford came and immediately sixteen mortars, ten heavy seige guns, eight field batteries and all the men of war and monitors, opened one of the most gigantic pyrotechnic displays that were witnessed during the war. Our land mortars in our seige operations, had gotten within a few hundred yards of the fort and formed a a crescent about the doomed stronghold, these and the vessels, two miles away, kept dropping their shells into the fort in front of us. From our position we could appreciate the unerring skill of the gunners who were sending these mighty missels of war in their archlike curves above our heads and dropping them invariably into the enemy's midst. What a grand sight to see those fiery balls rising behind us, sailing over us and dropping one by one, into the works in front. Imagine the dark curtain of night drawn about you while a hundred volcanoes are spitting fire and flame, a thousand thunders jaring the earth, the whole heavens above you filled with fiery messengers of death, all concentrated upon one small spot in which are bursting shells, magazines exploding the cheers of the living mingled with the groans of the dying while vast tongues of flames seathe, scorch and consume everything in their reach, and you have a picture of the twelve hours of the night of August 23, 1864, in Fort Morgan, Alabama.

After taking the fort we lay here a few days and then crossed over to the other side of the bay and landed upon Cedar Point, opposite to Fort Powell and upon the same side with the city of Mobile.

Upon this point we threw up some breast works and while so doing, we found a few pieces of artillery that the rebels had buried before they left and blew up Fort Powell. We had suffered from mosquitoes many times before, but never before had we met such large and blood thirsty ones as we found here; and after suffering from these by night and the broiling sun by day, until the 10th of September, when we boarded a steamer and left for New Orleans where we arrived on the 12th, but the next day we boarded the ram Switzerland, crossed over to Algiers and remained here until the 14th when we again embarked upon a steamer and moved up the river landing at Morganize Bend on the evening of the 14th.

CHAPTER VIII.

CONSOLIDATION—BATTLE OF FORT BLAKELY—END OF WAR.

> There sounded the tread of marching feet;
> Stately, slow, not the haste of retreat;
> Colors tossed high in the April breeze
> And kissed the budding forest trees.
> The drum had a voice not heard before;
> Its throbbing said: "We fight no more!
> We are coming home! Rejoice, Oh land!
> And thrill to the tread of each valiant band."

After landing at Morganzie Bend and pitching our tents we settled down to enjoy our comfortable quarters and a quiet camp life, but no sooner had we esconced ourselves in our comfortable quarters than, on the evening of the 19th of October we with two days rations in our haversacks and three in a wagon, as the darkness of the evening closed in, marched out to a bridge across a bayou where sometime previous the 26th Indiana had been captured.

We remained here guarding this bridge and occasionally drawing upon the country round about us for fresh meats, fowl, etc., for the good of the Union, until the 23rd, when on learning that the enemy on the Atchafalaya had left we marched back to camp at Morganzie, where we remained quietly in camp until Nov. 1st, when with ten days rations we again marched for the Atchafalaya, and when near said bayou we had a skirmish with the enemy, driving him back and across the bayou, when we moved up and took position upon the banks of this bayou.

On the morning of the 2d of Nov. skirmishing commenced up and down the bayou, in which Wm. Duckworth, of Co. G, with some others of our comrades were wounded.

This skirmishing was kept up vigorously from both banks of the bayou, and it was here that the rebels would fire a shell at us, and then cheer for McClelland while our batteries would return the compliment, by hurling shell at them, with cheers for Lincoln, so this desultory firing was kept up until the 9th, when we again marched back to our tents at Morganzie. Having lost two men killed and two wounded. We were now enjoying a quiet rest in our tents and all was going on pleasantly until the 12th, when Nelson Fielder, of Co. H, who was returning from picket duty, was shot dead by accident at his tent door. This incident cast a gloom over the whole camp, but our regiment never was given much time to brood over death or misfortune, but were allowed to drown our trouble in the arena of active warfare, so about 3 o'clock on the evening of the 18th we started for the Atchafalaya, and had gone about half way out, when the darkness and muddy roads compelled us to halt for the remainder of the night, but about 4 o'clock the next morning found us upon the move, while the great God of day began to light up these gloomy swamps. We found the enemy, and skirmishing commenced across the bayou, and we remained here fighting, foraging and destroying what the enemy might feed upon, until Oct. 29th, when we again returned to our quarters at Morganzie. We had now been marching and fighting near a month exposed to the weather, day and night, in sunshine and rain, while our tents stood peacefully twenty miles away, and now we returned to them and have one night's peaceful rest beneath their protecting folds and on the morning of Nov. the 1st, we strike tents and board the steamer Illinois, and started up the river to where or how far we knew not, but we soon come to Natches, halted a little while, then we moved on up the river passing Rodney, then Grand Gulf, when we stop a little while at our old battle ground, Vicksburg, but we soon moved on up the river, passing Lake Providence, and we finally landed at Shipper's landing where we take in tow a gunboat whose officers were under arrest for attempting to sell their boat to the enemy. We tow this boat on up passing Greenville and Columbia, and on Nov. 6th the 83rd Ohio and our regiment landed and went on an all nights scout, during which it rained a cold rain and on the next morning returned to our boats and moved up the river with our gun boat still in tow and during the day we took a little scout, but finding no enemy we proceeded up to White river landing, where we arrived on Nov. 8th., went into camp here with the understanding that we were to remain in winter quarters, and with all the energy known to a western army, we went to work, building huts out of logs and planks and making snug little quarters, having fireplaces and nice little chimneys and we finally had a model pioneer village, and settled down to regular housekeeping, but we were not allowed to enjoy the fruits of our labor, for on the 21st we again boarded the steamer and headed down stream leaving the pretty blue smoke curling up into the Heavens from the chimneys of our deserted village, while we retraced our voyage back to Morganzie Bend, where we again go into camp where we had left a few days ago. Now preparations were being made for our consolidation with the 24th Indiana, and as soon as this was done, we again, on Dec. 15, with the 24th Indiana and some colored troops boarded vessels and headed up the river accompanied by a few gunboats to Old River, where a short time previous some gunboat men had been decoyed off their boat by some ladies and where they on landing were shot and foully murdered by concealed rebels; and now we were sent here to retaliate by taking every man a prisoner of war, destroying all that an enemy could subsist upon, and thoroughly scourge the country, and to say that this was well done would faintly express it, for we loaded our boats with fresh meat inasmuch as to compel us to march overland back to camp, while our boats transported our spoils by the river. We returned to camp and remained there until Dec. 24th, when we broke camp and boarded a steamer, and went to Baton Rouge where we debarked and went into camp in the rear of the city for the first time. As the 24th Indiana, our regiment forming the left wing of this wing of this regiment, and as an independent organization the 67th passed out of existence, and the history of this regiment from now on to the end of the war is the history of the 24th Ind. as well. We remained here until the 29th of Dec., when we embarked and proceeded down the river and arrived at Carlton on the 30th where we went into camp near the shell road. Now under our new organization, Col. Spicely in command while Major Sears become Lieutenant Colonel of the 24th Ind., and since it is now holidays our discipline was slackened to some extent, and we had more privilege accorded us than usual, and while Gen. Canby was organizing his expedition against Mobile, we were enjoying the freedom of camp and city, except drills, inspection and reviews until the month of January and half of February had passed away when we broke camp and marched to Lake End, where we boarded a steamer and again passed down Lake Ponchartrain and out upon the waters of the Gulf, and turn eastward while our noble vessel is throbbing and trembling at every puff of steam, as though struggling to carry her precious freight through the foamy surf, to a port of safety. We passed Fort Gaines and Morgan, the scene of our twenty days battle, some six months before. We now skirted the coast of Florida until we reached Fort Barancas where we landed February 18th.

Now while the fragments of the 13th army corps, with three brigades of colored troops come to this place, the 16th army corps goes to Fort Morgan and while we make the trip through the pine forests of Florida, the 16th corps marches from Mobile Point to Spanish Fort, and while from the interior we come up in the rear of Fort Blakely the 16th corps are seiging Spanish Fort. After landing at Barrancus, we moved up into a nice pine grove, where we went into camp which was laid out in regular military style, with streets and alleys, which we surraced up and smoothed off, then we set out a row of fine shade trees on each side of the streets and mounded them up with deep yellow sand. And when all this was done we next laid out and constructed a music park amid the shady pines, in the midst of this park we erected a grand stand for the band. Now on the whole our camp looked like a fairy land, and when evening came on and the calm stillness of night had set in, our band from this grand stand discoarsed music like an angel band, upon the battlements of heaven while the whole world seemed to rejoice as we celebrated Washington's birthday.

But we were permitted to enjoy this fairy land but a little while and on March 13, we struck tents and marched about 20 miles through miry sand, when we came to Pensacola and went into camp near the old Ind. Fort, just above the city and here again we went to improving our quarters by tearing down the old deserted frame houses in the city and carrying them up and erecting quarters in our own modern style, and in a few days we had a densely populated model city, erected as by magic. But we had not more than got our city erected when on the 19th of March, with three days rations in our haversacks and five in a wagon, entered the depths of the pine forests of Florida, the whole army being now under command of Gen. Steele. We had moved but a little ways when it began to rain and continued to pour down all day while we kept plodding on hour after hour and having made but a few miles when night overtook us as wet as rats, with a poor chance of making a fire in these down pouring torrents, and our allowance of coffee fell short. As darkness closed in around us, the rain increased, and we could find no place to pitch our little dog tents, except upon the wet forest leaves. This wet night passed and morning came, the torrents seemed to have increased and we tried to make coffee upon a hundred little fires, that the rain quickly put out, then we rolled up our wet tents and blankets and packed up for the march, when it was discovered that our artillery and provision wagons could not be drawn, over that apparently sound surface, but would break through the crust and drop down ankle deep, when details from the army were put to pulling them out by hand, and now it was a novel sight to see hundreds of these wet soldiers pulling those wagons and cannons out of the mire, to go but a little ways when they again would break through and drop down to the axel, when the pulling process was again applied, and this kind of thing continued all day while the rain continued to pour down, and we had made but little progress, when night came on and overtook us in the same condition as the night before and we had to pitch our tents upon the wet earth and leaves, and our ration of coffee again fell short. During the night the rain ceased and when morning came the sun shone out most beautiful and warm, and by diligent searching we found enough pitch pine knots to make fires, and it was but a little while before the whole forests was full of those little fires, upon which sat many a tin cup and fruit can boiling the soldiers blessed beverage—coffee. Around these fires hung upon poles were hundreds and even thousands of wet and steaming blankets, while the whole canopy above seemed filled with dense black smoke, forming one of the most novel sights of the war. In the meantime our artillery and wagon teams were floundering and trying to pull their burdens, but making little or no progress, when Gens. Steele and Andrews concluded this progress was too slow, and determined to fell these tall pine trees, and make corduroy roads, so axes were brought up and brigade after brigade alternately were detailed to fell these pine trees, and cut them into twelve foot cuts, while hundreds of others were carrying these logs and laying them side by side. It was not long before thousands of axes were ringing in that lonely pine forest, and as handling tools was nothing new to the Hoosier boys, it was surprising how fast this road building progressed.

We had started out with but eight days rations, and our time was thus unexpectedly consumed and to be left in this interminable forest, cut off from all communication from the outside world was a position unenviable. This army of axe men continued their work, from day to day, until finally we struck a more solid terra firma, where the army came up and Gen. Lucas placed his cavalry in front, and again we resumed the march, but our eight days rations were about out and we were far from our destination, and to aggravate the care the rebels appeared in our front to dispute our further progress. But undaunted we pushed forward, pushing the enemy before us skirmishing each day and laying upon our arms at night, when we came up near the Escamby river, we came upon the rebels where Gen. Clanton of the Confederate army was shot through the body and our surgeon dressed his wounds and placed him in a hunter's cabin to die, but we learned afterwards that he got well. In capturing this man one of the 2d La. ordered him to surrender, and he replied that his name was not surrender and at the same time he drew a revolver and shot the man dead, in an instant a sergeant of the 2d La. shot Gen. Clanton through. We went into camp at this place for the night, and while gathering up wood for our camp fire, we captured several rebels, who had hidden themselves in the brush, thinking we would pass by without discovering them.

On the early morn we resumed the march, and after several hours marching came up to and went into camp near the Escamby river, and now that our eight days rations were so near exhausted that we were cut down to one cracker per day and since there was nothing in these pine forests to forage, our position became a little critical, and to aggravate the case the very atmosphere as well as the gum from the pine trees, sharpened up our appetites to a ravenous state, yet, without a murmur we moved along snathing the pine wax from the trees as we marched, and there never was a time in our history that we worked our jaws more vigorously.

On the following morning we were up and on the march early, and came up to the bridge of the Montgomery & Pensacola Ry., across the Escamby river, this bridge had been washed away except the stringers on one side, and the river

CROSSING THE ESCAMBIA RIVER.

was now full and raging leaving no way to cross but to coon these stringers, so here was another picturesque sight, to see these soldiers with knapsacks upon their backs, and rifle in hand, one after another, cooning these girders across these raging waters, but in due time our whole division were across and with Gen. Andrew, at at our head formed column and moved up toward Pollard a few miles from the river, and on nearing the town we were formed by divisions into columns at a right shoulder shift, presenting a fine sight, as we moved through these tall pine woods. On arriving at the city limits we deployed into line of battle, encircling the city and closed in upon it, but on arriving there, we found the rebels had gone, and no one there except a few old women. Here we captured a rebel commissary, with a quantity of bean crackers which was a timely capture, and we lost no time in appropriating them to the cause of the Union, then we went to work tearing up the Montgomery and Mobile Ry. by turning it over like sod before a plow, twisting the rails and burning the ties while on the other end of the road we found a steam engine with fire yet in the furnace, just as the rebels had left it in their flight, we got up steam and sent it whizzing and snorting into rebeldom, then we burned down the rebel commissary and resumed our march, coming to the river we again performed the cooning process, and by night we were all over and we joined the main army where we had left them in the morning.

Now we went into camp for the night, and on the morrow we found it raining, but resumed our march at an early hour, and continued marching all day through mud and rain, our clothes and blankets becoming thoroughly soaked, rendering marching extremely laboring, but when night came on and the darkness gathered about us forming an impenetrable dungeon, while the torrents still pouring down, we continued to feel our way on and on, each man feeling for his file leader in front and thus we continued feeling and groping our way through this midnight darkness, and torrents of rain until about 3 o'clock in the morning when we halted and dropped down in place to rest for the remainder of the night.

Next morning the sun rose bright and warm, while the birds of the forests were singing their morning song, the steam could be seen rising from these tired exhausted men as they lay in long rows where they had dropped a few hours before while the soft tropical breezes were fanning their fevered brows, and the golden rain drops were twingling and dancing and falling like the tears of heaven upon these exhausted patriots. After the sun had been up some time this sleeping army was awakened and having but little breakfast to prepare we dried ourselves by the fire and sunshine as best we could, for a few hours, and then moved up a few miles to a landing on the edge of the upper bay where we halted and bathed, and rested till the following morning when at an early hour we were on the move upon the road to Blakely.

The enemy being near, our march was necessarily slow, but we had by this time exhausted all our rebel crackers and and were anxious to open communication with A. J. Smith for supplies, so we pushed on until about 3 o'clock in the evening of April the 5th when by division into column and at a right shoulder shift, with band in front we went right up in front of Fort Blakely upon whose works we could see the great glistening guns beaming down upon us in a very forbidding manner, but we deployed into line of battle, and moved up to a little ravine in front of these great batteries when we halted and immediately sent a detail around to Smith's corps for rations which, just at night came up and again we had plenty of hardtack and coffee.

We established our lines and put out our picket lines when the rebels opened fire and raked the ground over which we had just passed, but we had bivouacked in line of battle for the night and though the cannon boomed and the shells screemed we slept and rested for the morning. Now on arriving at Blakely, the colored troops were placed on the extreme right while our regiment was next to them, while the remainder of

FORT BLAKELY.

the division were in line on our left, and we now opened a regular seige and keeping a constant fire from our batteries and pickets by day and moving up a little at night digging rifle pits and pickets holes at each stop, but as the process of seige had been described in the foregoing pages of this work we will abreviate, by stating that by the evening of the 8th we had pushed our line up so near the rebel lines that we could see their tents and flags behind their works. As the evening sun was sinking behind the western horizon and a beautiful soft calm twilight and a quiet reigned throughout both camps, suddenly the rebel band in our front struck up the tune, "Bonnie Blue Flag" which came floating upon the balmy breezes across the battle field and echoed among the hills and forests in sweet strains worthy of a better cause. When this had ceased a perfect silence reigned over the two armies for a space of a few moments when our 24th Indiana Reg. band struck up the "Star Spangled Banner" which seemed to reverberate throughout the armies and echo from hill to hill and from pine to pine, filling the whole atmosphere with sweet strains of patriotic music, while evening spread her curtain of darkness over both armies; and that music had settled down into the hearts of both friend and foe, leaving the rebels in silent thought while from the union lines, from thousands of patriotic throats, came cheer after cheer, and all was quiet and deathly stillness reigned, while both blue and gray lay down to think of home and friends. And thus ended the last tune played by any Confederate band

But little did the gray think that the next evening would find them prisoners of war and the last battle for their cause fought and lost while the protecting folds of the Star Spangled Banner would wave over all rebeldom.

The morning of the 9th of April found us near to the rebel works and all our batteries in position. Musket firing and bombarding from our batteries were going on and the rebels were filling the air about us with deadly missiles, continuing thus until the afternoon, when a partial calm ensued. At 4 o'clock Gen. Granger ordered the whole line to advance some hundred yards to the front and halt and dress our lines. But no sooner had we started to that position when a hurrah burst forth and our regiment rushed forth. The yell was caught up on our left, and then from the dusky throats of the colored troops it was heard, and now the whole line from right to left like a storm cloud rushed on and over a line of torpedoes through an abattis of pine trees knit together by wire, and we were pitching plunging and scrambling through this wire and brush while the rebels were pouring grape and cannister, and the bullets were pattering around us like rain, while the air was filled with sulphurous smoke, shouts and groans. But through this storm of death we rushed on up to and into the ditch, then up to and into the fort, when white flags came forth all along the line. Just then a tremendous noise was heard on our right, and on looking in that direction we saw the rebels coming like vapor before a storm, while the colored troops were close upon them like a black cloud, shooting, sticking and knocking the rebels and shouting at the top of their voices, "Fort Pillow! Fort Pillow."

The rebels had refused to surrender to these colored troops, and they, in retalliation for the Fort Pillow massacre did not wish them to surrender, and were coming upon them like infuriated demons, making it necessary for the white troops to go to the rescue of the retreating rebels. Soon order was restored and the last battle of the war was fought.

We immediately moved up and camped upon the battle-ground. While here, on the 12th of April, we heard of Lee's surrender at Appomattox, which created one of the most enthusiastic and joyful jollifications that we ever witnessed.

It was late in the evening when all were sitting about their camp fires with the curtains of darkness drawn about us and the stars in the blue vaults of heaven, as it were, began to come forth and take their places upon the ampitheatre while the soft spring breezes among the pines were playing

the tune of the Gods These patriots where sitting about
their flickering camp fires talking over the past, the present,
and the future, when we should see home and friends, when
suddenly came floating on the still calm air on our right, cheer
after cheer, and like a tidal wave it flew from regiment to
brigade and from brigade to division until it pervaded the
whole army and the air was filled with long and loud cheers,
which seemed to make the whole earth tremble and the pine
trees to quiver in an ecstacy of joy, while the old veterans
were crying like children, while one of the grandest handshak-
ings took place that it is possible for humans to witness,
while the hours of the night flew past without rest or sleep,
and on the next morning our flag seemed to flutter with new
lustre and life and everybody seemed to be happy invigorated
with the thought of home and friends whom we should soon
meet, but we were not destined to enjoy such happiness without some clouds of sorrow, and while we yet remained upon
the same battlefield where we had fought the last battle of
the war, and where we had received the glorious news of
Lee's surrender, in the midst of our rejoicing a dark cloud of
sorrow came over our sky like a cyclone whose message on
the wings of lightning came like a thunder bolt that paralyz-
ed our hops and deadened our joys with the message, "Lincoln is assassinated!" This spread a dark cloud of sorrow
upon our whole camp, and the tears of joy were turned into
tears of sorrow, while dark looks of vengeance settled upon
the brows of those brave patriots who were now here and
there, gathered in little groups with tear stained faces, talking in low mutterings. And so continued hour after hour until
the god of day hid his face and refused to shine, and drew a
cloud of mourning over our sorrow-stricken camp, which settled down into a low humming of sorrow and vengeance, while
the wind through the pine trees seemed to play their Aeolian
tunes of mourning to the vigils of heaven.

    Thus we were in a few short hours transported to the
highest pinnacle of joy and hurled to the lowest vale of sor-

row. But our three years of warfare had taught us to fight the battles of life as well as of war, as we came to them, and with sorrow in our hearts and doubts in our minds time passed on and on, and on the 20th we marched down the bay and embarked for Selma, Ala., and picking our way between the buoys planted there to guard us off of Rebel torpedoes, we wended our way across the bay to the city of Mobile, which had been evacuated on our capturing Fort Blakely. Halting here and waiting long enough for the formation of a fleet of thirteen transports loaded with the 2d Division of the 13th Army Corps and three brigades of colored troops, preceeded by gunboats with torpedo rakes in their front, we, on the 22d left the city and moved up the Alabama River, slowly and cautiously, traveling by day and laying up at night. On reaching the up river the country become very broken and the river very narrow, while the high bluffs jutted right up to the river banks. One morning, when all were moving along quietly, from the tops of one of those bluffs was seen a little puff of smoke, a report of a rifle was heard and a bullet struck and killed a man on the top of one of our boats. Gen. Steele at once ordered a halt and landing sent a squad of calvary in pursuit of the assassin, but to no avail, he could not be found. Steele then placed posters on trees and other public places, stating that if another man was killed he would devastate the whole country.

Here, piled up beneath a tree not far from the river we found quite a lot of bacon, for which no owner could be found. We assumed guardainship over it and loaded it upon our boats for the good of the union, and again resumed our trip up the river. On arriving at Cahaba we landed for a little while and found that most of the citizens were gone, leaving the women and negroes in possession, and while we were taking in the city some negroes informed us of a couple of yankees locked up in a cellar to starve to death. To this place we hurried and found the door locked, but we soon burst it down and to our horror found two living skeletons lying there starving to death. We took them to the boat and fed them little by little with a spoon, so near dead were they.

On making this discovery, in order to save the city from flames and utter destruction, Steele was compelled to order us all aboard immediately. This order, only, saved the city from ruin and destruction.

When on board we again moved up the river until the 27th when we arrived at Salma, when we embarked and went into camp just in the rear of the city. Here we found in the hospital several Indiana comrades, who were wounded while taking the place, and on the outskirts of the city we found where Wilson had burned down foundries that had been turning out cannons for the Confederate army and navy during the whole war, where now a great many unfinished cannon lay, as relics of the lost cause.

This we found to be a nice and well laid out city, more like northern cities than any we had yet seen, having nice parks and straight and shady streets, but the people were yet bitter rebels and displayed only a poor show of friendship to the union soldiers.

The war was now over and the confederate armies were now disbanding and coming home, humiliated and chagrined over their defeat. It was feared that many depradations and outbreaks might occur unless there was protection from the government. Hence we were here to protect the life and property of our defeated foe. While here rebel soldiers were constantly coming in from their broken up armies and the city was soon full of gray uniforms. Notwithstanding the war was over we had never slackened our discipline, as to drills uniforms and acoutrement, but on the contrary, all took pride in exhibiting to the ex-rebels our proficiency in drills, especially the manual of arms. At our evening parades thousands of Longstreet's men and others, with ladies and citizens, crowded to the grounds to witness the yankees practice the art of war, which seemed to astonish them, while they stood or sat in grum silence. But from some of Longstreet's men we received many encomiums of soldiery praise.

While here Gen. A. J. Smith reviewed our 13th Corps and this was the last grand review the 13th Army Corps ever had. On the morning of the 11th of May we broke camp and while our 24th Reg. band made the very trees on the sidewalks dance with loyalty, we followed them to the river, where we embarked for Mobile.

Nothing of any special note occurred on this trip and the river being clear of obstructions, we made good headway and landed at Mobile on May 14th and went into camp in a beautiful grove in the rear of the city where our wounded and invalids of the Blakely campaign rejoined us.

During our stay here a great explosion occurred at the wharf which sounded like a mighty earthquake, and seemed to shake the earth to its very center. Some of our boys being in the city at the time, received injuries from which they never recovered. We still kept up our discipline and parades, and one evening while on dress parade, it was lightning and sharp claps of thunder were rending the air, as to make it dangerous to hold dress parade under our glittering bayonets. Lieutenant Colonel Sears ordered us to break ranks, and we had but returned to our tents when a vivid flash of lightening came blinding us as in a blaze of fire, while there was a deafening thunderbolt crashed among the pines, hurling a shower of limbs upon our tents. We soon found that the lightning had struck a pine and run down, killing a man and wounding several others of Co. E. The rain came down in blinding torrents, and we laid the wounded out in this dashing rain, which hastened their recovery.

By this time our proficiency in the art of war had become a theme of conversation even in our own army and among the citizens of Mobile. So when it was noised about that on a certain day we would hold dress parade and go through the manual of arms in the public park, when that day came soldiers, citizens, ladies and ex-Confederates, blocking up every available space, while the ever present peanuts climbed the trees. Promptly at the hour and minute we entered the park, when from the Union soldiers thundered forth cheers, while the citizens and Confederates sat still and mute. Here is what a rebel paper had to say of this parade:

"Among the many fine regiments composing the 13th Army Corps, we have seen no one which in drill, soldiery bearing, and indeed, in all that goes to make a fine body of soldiers, surpasses the 24th and 67th Indiana Volunteers. On last Saturday the Regiment held a dress parade in the park of this city, and we repeat but the voice of the hundreds of spectators who witnessed it, when we say the Regiment acquitted itself in a manner alike creditable to itself, to its state and to its gallant Colonel (W. T. Spicely) who drilled it, and brought it to its present high state of perfection in the Art Militare."

During the war we have seen many fine regiments, among them First Regular and the celebrated 11th Ind., but we know of none which can excell the 24th in drill, particularly in the manual of arms. On Sunday evening the regiment went through the different movements with a uniformity and precision which enlisted the highest econiums from the spectators, citizens and officers of other commands. The "Order Arms," "Present Arms," "Right Shoulder Shift" were especially superb.

The regiment on this occasion was commanded by Lieutenant Col. F. A. Sears, a brave and daring officer. Not the least interesting entertaining feature of the performance was the excellent music furnished by the regimental band. We were glad to known that the 24th Regiment is in good health and numbers nearly 900.

We remained here until June 28th, when we again broke camp and marched down to the wharf to embark for a voyage across the Gulf of Mexico to Galveston, Texas. On arriving at the wharf we discovered that our vessel from the ocean was too large to make a landing here, and we were to be conveyed to her on a small vessel which soon came up to the shore and we embarked upon it. By this time night came on and with it heavy clouds, and long before we reach ed our ocean vessel, out on the bay, all the sailors were flying from rig to rig, tightening down ropes and furling sails, and preparing for a storm, in the meantime the dark clouds hovered above us and total darkness set in, while the heavy swells silently and sullenly followed each other, while the blinding lightning lit up the watery deep and the thunder seemed almost to shake out the bottom of the deep beneath us. But after a while we reached our ocean ship, the Hudson, and came up along side for transfer, but the rolling waves beneath us kept the ships bobbing up and down so much that it was impossible for all to jump from one vessel to another and only a part succeeded in getting aboard, the rest remaining on the little vessel while the storm passed off without much danger, so on June the 29th after we were safely transferred to the Hudson—an old Austrian wooden sail vessel, which we captured at Wilmington, N. C., and we might say that this ended the list of different kinds of vessels that we, during our service, had rode upon. Having rode upon every kind of vessel known to war or fisheries or the commerce of the U. S.

Our sails being unfurled and bellied out we headed due south till well out upon the water of the great Gulf, when we turned west and nothing of importance occurring until we arrived to a point opposite the mouth of the Mississippi when it was discovered that our supply of fresh water had run short and we were compelled to run up into the Mississippi to replenish our stock of fresh water. When we again set sail the wind had increased in its fury until now the great blue waves were running uncomfortably high and so were the contents of our stomachs, and it was a laughable sight, at each lurch of the vessel to see how liberally we would contribute to the great drove of sharks that were continually following us. But undaunted the boys would climb the rope ladders, and sway to and fro while the great foamy waves would splash across the hurricane deck, while the old tars would say that we were the dambdest set of land lubbers they ever saw. All went well as we tacked our way across the green mountain-like waves that were threatening to break our vessel into in the middle as screeching and cracking was heard as she sat at right angles across the great foam capped waves.

On July 1st, we arrived off Galveston some 12 miles where we anchored, our vessel being two heavy to pass over the bar, hence another transfer from ship to land which was done by a small gunboat. When safely landed we moved out in the rear of the city, and went into camp where our dress parade still go on as usual, but no picket nor camp guard and since Kirby Smith had surrendered our camping here was like a military picnic, as every rebel armed force had now surrendered and our time being about out we were anxiously awaiting the time to come when we should set sail for home, so on the 19th of July just three years from date of enlistment, our discharges were made out, many of the boys retaining their old Springfield rifles that had proved faithful upon many battle fields. But we were not to receive our pay until we reached Indianapolis, and having been with the 24th now nearly six months and in the service of the U. S. for three years we were on this day to sever our connection with the 24th and from the military service of the United States forever.

Having entered into the service with one thousand men, and having fought 29 battles and many skirmishes and having traveled over nine of the so-called Confederate States, and having traveled as much as once around the earth and having been under fire 170 days, and now with only 236 scar worn veterans left we severed our connection from the armies of the United States and prepared to meet the battle of civil life as citizens of a mighty Republic.

So we boarded the steamer St. Mary and crossed the Gulf, which at this time is as smooth as a floor and once more ascend the great father of waters to New Orleans where after waiting a short time for transportation we again boarded an old inferior transport which was liable to blow up at any moment and being ordered to Jeffersonville, In l., we remained upon this boat until we reached Cairo. Ill., when the 94th Ill.

debarked and we went off with them and refused to go further upon that old inferior boat when after some parleying a telegram was sent to Gov. Morton, and he being informed of the fact, immediately ordered us by rail to Indianapolis, so we soon boarded a freight train and came on up to within a few miles of Greencastle where the floods had carried away a bridge and we debarked and lay in a beech woods until late in the evening when Gov. Morton brought a passenger train to convey us to the city, where on the next day—Aug. 4th –the citizens gave us a fine reception supper, and we were welcomed by the thousands of citizens and by hundreds of ladies with tears trickling down their cheeks. And here we now disband forever.

A Secret Voyage on the Lower Mississippi and Gulf Coast,

By COL. R. B. SCOTT, Bedford, Ind.

After remaining in parole camp in the lower part of New Orleans from the 1st of January, 1864, to about the 20th of March when we were moved out to Lake End, (Now East End) some six miles out in the rear of the city where we encamped upon the lake shore and remained in a state of inactivity until about June 1st, and like all bodies of volunteer soldiers we became very restless and impatient at our state of inactivity and long deferred exchange, and any diversion whatever that would offer a change would be gladly welcomed.

Just about this time an incident did occur that offered a few of us an opportunity for a little diversion.

Now at the time Gen. Butler captured New Orleans all the small sailing crafts upon the Gulf coast, Lakes Bolixia, Bowen and Ponchurtrain were taken across to the rebel side of these waters and remained in possession of the enemy and up to this time—April, 1864, our authorities had been much annoyed by the smuggling of supplies, provisions and information across these waters to the enemy by means of these small sailing crafts, which larger boats could not follow the devious winding ways through these many narrow channels. But now Gen. W. T. Sherman being in command of this post, determined to put a stop to this source of annoyance, so the evening of April 19th there came to our quarters a call for eight volunteers to perform some secret and dangerous duty and Sherman, rather than have a detail made, called for the volunteer services of eight willing men. Jacob Payne, James L. Anderson, Howard Cordell, Geo. Collins, Wilson Morris and the writer, (all of the 67th Ind.,) jumped at this opportunity for a change and volunteered at once, for a duty the nature of which we knew nothing, but we at once received orders to report at Gen. Sherman's headquarters at 9 o'clock on the following morning for instructions.

On the morning of the 20th of April, at the appointed hour we with much anxiety and impatience to know what the nature of the duty was, reported, and to our surprise received the following order: "Go to Algiers, (just across the river from New Orleans) where on dock, you will find a small sailing smack, called the "Liza Jane," launch her, rig her up and provision her for an extended cruise, take her down the Mississippi river into the gulf, then cruise around the gulf coast eastward through bays and channels to Lake Ponchurtrain, thence up to rear of the city, being careful to note the depth, width and general direction of the various channels and inlets and bayous and report a diagram of the same to these headquarters." We then received the following passport: "The Post quartermaster is instructed to furnish the bearers with all necessary supplies of whatsoever nature, upon the requisition of said bearers, and gunboats, forts or commands are hereby instructed to pass and render whatever assistance the bearers may need in carrying out their instructions." To say that we were astonished at these orders would but feebly express it, to think that we Hooiser boys who had never been upon a stream larger than White river and had never manned a boat larger than a skiff or dugout, now ordered to launch, rig and mann a sailing brig, and venture upon the great Gulf was a thought preposterous, but then anything for a change.

So leaving headquarters at 10 o'clock we immediately proceeded to Algiers and after some considerable search found the Liza Jane, a pretty good hull, but nothing else, and now one of the puzzling problems of our life came, but fortunately for us, there were some idle sailors there at the time who willingly assisted us in making out a bill of fixtures necessary for the full rigging of our vessel and with this bill we proceeded to the quartermasters office and drew everything we needed such as ropes, block and tackle, oars, sails, masts and a stove and a good supply of rations and finally a mariner's compass and a blank log book, of this book we knew just about as much as of the other fixtures.

The Liza Jane was high up on dock and the next thing was to launch her and of course, like all the other things we knew how to do this, any boy in Indiana would know as much, but through the valuable suggestions of the sailors, we constructed a track and soaped it and then all got hold and we heaved and set then set and heaved, then she screeches and moves, slowly at first, then faster and faster she goes and finally strikes the water and shoots out upon the bosom of the Mississippi; many thanks to the jack tars, and our first difficult job being successfully accomplished and night being upon us, we suspended operations until morning when we finished the rigging process and supplied our boat with everything necessary, as we thought, but just as we were about to embark it was discovered that in making out requisitions, we had ommitted to include a flag and it would never do to sail without a flag, so we hastily procured one and hoisted it upon the top of the mast pole and then embarked, loosened the cable, hoisted the sails and shoved off under the fluttering stars and strips and amid cheers from the sailors on shore we headed down the great and muddy stream which filled our hearts with doubt and anxiety.

When we reached the middle of the river and sailed a few miles a breeze sprang up and the waves ran uncomfortably high and our boat groaned under her weight of wind causing us a degree of uneasiness, when we were halted by a post river guard on the out post who ordered us to round in and report, but we did not have sufficient command of our vessel to make her do our bidding as readily as old sailors and instead of rounding in we just simply slackened sail and let our boat drift with the current and compelled the captain of the guard to come to us. This ignorantly showed him our independence and when the captain scaned our passport he seemed to not understand the matter—in fact no one did except

Gen. W. T. Sherman, the quartermaster and ourselves—and after scrutenizing us closely and inspecting our ship load, found nothing suspicious, but had he looked beneath some canvass in the hole, he would have found Enfield rifles and navy revolvers which we had taken with us, contrary to instructions, but he could not understand, why just eight soldiers should go out into an enemies country unarmed and unequipped, but there was Gen. Sherman's handwriting, he dared not disobey, and we would not make any definite explanation, so he reluctantly let us pass, and on we moved beyond the union lines into an unknown country, where at any moment a puff of blue smoke on the banks might send a missile of death without a moments warning. Night came on and we tied up and went on shore to camp for the night.

> Where we boiled our coffee,
> And fried our bread
> Neath the cypress trees,
> Where ne'er a Yankee trod.

After the hard days anxiety and excitement rest was highly appreciated and when night spread her sable curtain of darkness about us we lay down in the arms of Morpheus, when the horrid silence of night set in, broken only by the low murmur of the restless deep, mixed now and then with the doleful sighing breeze through the mournful woods, and our rest was broken occasionally by the bellowing of Alligators and the ever ready Gallinipper. So our first night out was spent, and with the morning we were ready to untie and shove out as the sun rose.

Now the river being two narrow for sail vessels and now amid calms and adverse winds, we could make but poor headway, being compelled to tack and retack and cross and recross the river so many times that on the second day we concluded to tie up about 3 o'clock and then proceed to explore the adjacent country. We had been here but a little while when there appeared a full-blooded, long-haired Louisana citizen gorilla, innocently sauntering about for awhile and inquiring if we intended remaining there over night, if so he he had some oranges he wished to trade for coffee. We informed him that we might trade some and he left for the interior to bring up his oranges and the evening passed away while our long haired friend failed to show up, however about sundown there appeared another one of Louisana's product, similar to the first and entered a protest against our remaining there over night, but we told him that we had concluded to stay, as we were in no particular hurry and after some little growling he left us, but in about half an hour four specimens of the same product appeared and demanded that we leave, we informed them that we had put in there to stay, that we were under that flag floating at the mast pole and intended to stay all night, that we did not intend to burn any one's houses, steal anything nor to kill any one if we were unmolested, but in the event we were we would not be responsible for results. While this conversation was going on some of our boys brought forth our Enfields and stacked them upon the bank, which seemed to annoy our visitors—what pursuasive powers have these Enfields when properly handled—who after some grumbling and murmuring, left, but we did not know how soon to return, nor how many others they might bring with them. So we made ready for emergencies by lengthening out our cabel, examining our revolvers and placing our Enfields conveinent for use.

After eating our supper and arranging for sentinels we lay down to sleep, no not sleep, for there was a spirit of wakfulness upon us which seemed to stay with us all the night. Though we could hear little disturbances off aways, nothing approached us more dangerous than those ever present bloodthirsty gallinippers. Morning came pretty and bright and we disembarked and made up a big fire on shore and cooked and ate our breakfast and then loitered around there until near 9 o'clock, we would have left early but to show our independence we remained awhile to see what we should see.

No enemy put in appearance so we spread our sails and moved out into and down the river and soon came to that long and narrow strip of land on each side of the river extending far out into the gulf. Across this narrow strip we could see the great blue waters of the gulf extending into great briny fields as far as the eye could see and when we beheld these great foam crested waves and then looked at our little "Liza Jane" we must acknowledge that we had no little misgivings about our hearts and to add to this our citizen pilot acknowledged that he knew but little of the route over which our mission lay, we had some mistrust about this citizen all the time and now our suspicions were strengthened and it seemed too bad to have our pilot fail us just at the time we were to commence the work of our mission. Just now we have an insight of Forts Phillips and Jackson which guards the mouth of the Mississippi and on arriving within a couple of miles of the Forts we went ashore for a council of war, it then being so calm that we could make no headway sailing.

This was about noon and we lay here all evening and night during which we explored and scouted up and down the narrow strip of land upon which were some fine orange groves, nice and beautiful to behold. During our scout we came upon a fisherman's hut where we found an honest, intelligent old fisherman who possessed a knowledge of all the coast and waters which we wished to explore, and after some hard persuasion we prevailed on him to accompany us upon our voyage. As a compensation we agreed to give him a check upon the quartermaster at New Orleans for $20 and were to board him while with us, thus we had superceded the citizen pilot given us by Gen. Sherman and substituted the fisherman. But we had no thought of sending away this citizen pilot, but determined that he should accompany us to add ornament to our society, and now all being satisfactorily arranged we prepared for our venture upon the briny deep, and in conversation with our new pilot we discovered that some distance above Fort Jackson there was a narrow cut off from the river through to Hog Island Bay, through which small vessels sometimes could pass and by going through this pass we could save some 40 or 50 miles, so we determined to try the cut off and accordingly dropped down and across the river and soon found said pass, and on examination found it as represented by our fisherman, but the water was too shallow for our craft to sail through, but we determined to tow her through with ropes, so leaving the most of our clothing on board, and like mules upon a tow path soon pulled our Liza Jane into this narrow ditch and by a great deal of hard pulling we finally got to tide waters on Hog Island Bay upon whose waters we launched out, running out the jib and unfurling the main sail which now caught the wind and we sped out upon the water while the boys sang:

> "Get along Liza Jane, get along &c."
> "How glorious her gallant course she goes,
> Her white wings flying—never from her foes;
> She walks the waters like a thing of life,
> Who would not brave the battle—fire—the wreck,
> To move the monarch of her peopled decks."

We had sailed but a little ways when we suddenly struck a shoal and our vessel was likely to ground at any moment, and we were compelled to reef sail and draw in the jib, go slow and feel our way. But this was what we were here for and we note it down, this shoal was full of young oysters, which hatch here and continue to grow until the next rise in the Mississippi, when its fresh waters flow over here and kills them. We procured some of these oysters by getting out and grabbing them up with our hands.

We spent the evening feeling and creeping along till now we were out of sight of land except now and then a small island.

These islands were covered with rank grass in which sea gulls lay their eggs and raise their young and our fisherman told us that in May of each year one could procure bushels of eggs here by burning the rank grass, we thought this would be novel as well as interesting, if we could be fortunate enough to meet with good luck and as the evening was far spent, the sun sank down behind the western waters and night came on and we hove up to a small island and anchored, we did not tie up as we did while on the river where the water was too deep for our anchor.

This island but a few rods across and covered with rank dry grass seemed to be a good field to hunt sea birds eggs upon. so after supper when darkness had gathered about us in solid black walls, while we were many miles from friend or foe and miles from the mainland, while the stars of heaven were piercing the midnight darkness with their electric spark and the phosphorescent fishes were lighting up the waters about us and our little ship bobbing up and down on the silent waters like a bird with folded wings, at rest. We formed a skirmish line around the island with match in hand and simultaneously the blaze sprang up in liquid flames like the firey tongue of the God of fire, filling the vaults of heaven with great columns of black smoke and driving the darkness behind us in solid walls of inky blackness. while each opposite face dressed in a firey garb, looked like imps from the infernal regions.

After witnessing this grand spectacle and the flames had died out, we went aboard our little ship and retired for the night and tossed and rocked to sleep by the gentle rolling swells of the briny deep which kept ebbing and flowing all night, and so we passed our first night upon the trustless main.

Early next morning we arose and went forth, bareheaded, in search for our sea eggs for breakfast, but unfortunately for us it was too early in the season and the birds had not yet commenced laying and we had no eggs for breakfast, but we consoled ourselves by saying that the grand picturesque firey scene had paid us for our trouble. In the midst of this small circular island we found a square cut stone set up like a small tombstone and our thoughts immediately ran back to the days of Captain Kidd. Why this stone was placed here we knew not, nor did we hesitate to find out, but returned to our boat, ate breakfast, weighed anchor and were soon pursuing our journey over the beautiful placid waters, feeling our way, sounding channels and noting position of islands; this duty was all the writer had to perform, and all day, sounding first this channel then that one, noting this island then that one, and nothing of interest or importance occurring. We crossed the greater portion of what is locally called the Mississippi Sound, when night came on and we anchored out upon the briny deep with no land near and ate our supper, when the ever ready pipe was brought forth and a social group sat upon the deck enjoying this romantic scene, while the sun had, as it were, sank into a watery grave, leaving a firey hue to the western horizon which cast a rich mellow hue upon the surrounding waters, while the dark daily circle was climbing the western sky, seating the celestial visitors upon the ampitheatre of heaven and the soft evening breeze was rolling the darkblue swells about us while the phosphorescent fishes were shooting hither and thither in the depths beneath us, making it delightful to sit there and listen to our fisherman's stories and superstitions. He there, in the beautiful scene, saw signs of a pending storm, but we, caring nothing for signs or superstitions made light of his predictions, but he with a solemn air upon his countenance, ominiously shook his head and finally the hours wore away and we retired for the night.

Next morning after the usual routine, we weighed anchor and with a fine breeze, we had a clear sailing over the depths which our sounding line could not measure, finding but few islands, hence but few channels. The coast off to our left was but a continuous shallow lagoon or swamp, the habitation a mulitude of aligators with which we had no particular business and with fine sailing we moved on and on league after league, when suddenly off to our left there came up from the depths of the sea, some great sea animal, such as we had never seen before, but its stay upon the surface was so brief we could not determine what it looked like, some saying it looked like a cow, while others said it was a sea horse. Now our fisherman was sitting silent with a troubled look upon his brow, but we kept a look out for the monster to reappear. when just then one came up off to our right and soon others by two and fours came up and went back. By this time the old faithful Enfield was brought forth and some one shot one of these animals. This struck the fisherman with horror he said that these animals were porpoises and were the sailors friends and came up to warn us of an impending storm and to hurt one of these was to offend the God of storms and he in his trouble, insisted upon us going to land and wait till the storm was over, but we told him that we cared not for the porpoises nor the storm God. This seemed to almost paralyze him with horror, but we sped on, having our jokes and fun while the old fisherman remained blue, and he studied what kind of material a yankee was made of not to fear God or Devil.

After sailing awhile, away off to our right in the distance we spied a sail and for curiosities sake, headed that way and increasing our speed by putting out our jib and giving more belly to the main sail, so on we went while the boys sang. "Get along Liza Jane." Now our newly discovered sail saw us heading for her and sheared off to the right and increased her speed and then this act of running from us made us the more anxious to catch up with her, so we put our Liza Jane to her utmost speed while the strange vessel was now doing her best to out run us and so now we had a fine race over these to us, unknown waters, and we now, according to the rules of the navy, ran up the stars and stripes, which fluttered as we sped along like a thing of life, and we were gaining on the stranger. Yes the distance between us was growing less and less and the excitement was growing intense and our Enfields and navys were placed in convient places. See how she hugs that island! She is trying to ground us, sheer off boys, sheer off! See, she is in the trap she has set for us, she is aground! See how they work tug and pull. But it is of no use, she is fast and we have the channel. Cheer up boys, plank her, ah, we glide around her within rifle shot.

By the motion of their hands and hats we knew they would surrender. Now this capturing of a vessel was something unlooked for as we had instructions to take no arms with us but now our devilment had got us into trouble and we must put on an official look and get out of it. But here we had an elephant upon our hands in the shape of a captured vessel, which we did not know how to get rid of. But after a short council of war we agreed to accept the surrender and with a long and authoritive face, we moved up slowly and cautiously until we could speak to them, and to our surprise we found the crew were Spaniards and could not speak the English language. This added another perplexity to our predicament, but fortunately the writer had a smattering of the Spanish language at that time, and we accepted the surrender and it turned out that they were not rebels, but foreigners who had obtained a fishing pass and had let its time run out, for renewal and by reason of this they mistrusted we were after them and when the stars and stripes appeared they were sure of it, hence their run. So with the solemnity and red tape known to West Point or the navy, we accepted the surrender and it will be remembered that we had let no one loose since we started, lest they go to the enemy and report who we were and the mission we were upon, even our citizen pilot we kept along after his discharge. This new capture had four men aboard and we took vessel and crew along with us during the remainder of the day and when night came on we anchored and kept a close watch upon our capture and the next morning we released it upon the condition that the crew would report immediately at New Orleans and renew their pass and that we should take their pilot with us to a point upon Lake Bowen, and would leave him upon a certain island and they should follow next day and pick him up. This was agreed to especially by us, and we moved off with the jolly Spaniard as hostage on board, leaving the Spanish vessel to follow next day and at the time of leaving this Spanish vessel and crew we expected to be at the island agreed upon to leave our hostage, at the appointed time, but finding more work, and devious winding ways, than we anticipated we did not arrive there until the evening of the second day, and we had a very pleasant time cruising among these emerald Isles and when we did arrive we found our Spanish crew uneasy and anxiously awaiting the delivery of their pilot, they had become uneasy lest the Yankees had played them a trick. After cooking and eating our supper, it being a clear bright evening, and there being a fair sailing breeze, and being informed by our pilot that by sailing in a southeast direction we would soon come in sight of the light house at Fort Pike, though it had not been our custom to sail after night, as our business did not admit of it, but now our mission was ended, we concluded to take a sail that night, so embarking and setting our sails to the wind we bade our Spaniards a final adieu and headed toward Lake Bowen.

The evening shades had now hovered about us and the darkness had settled upon the dark and turbid waters about us, while the soft spring sea breeze carried the echoes of that merry song—"Get along Liza Jane," far out upon the still waters. After singing this merry song until it became stale and the dark calmness seemed to settle down impressively upon the boys, we all settled down to a silent meditation and while our noble Liza Jane was plowing the briny waters, we enjoyed our own thoughts in this silent and beautiful calmness and while we were enjoying the scene our old fisherman was brooding over the porpoise episode and said a storm was sure to overtake us.

After sailing awhile we have an insight of the lighthouse at Fort Pike, which seemed very small and apparently down in the water, even the gentle swells would hide it from view, our pilot told us this was the lighthouse and adjusted the sails accordingly. Let out our sails and adjusted the boom and sped on like a thing of life, hour after hour, while the light ahead grew larger and higher up and in due time we could see the outlines of land ahead and upon the one hand we knew were union lines, while on the other were the rebel lines and on one side was nothing but a continuous line of swamps, while on the other side, near and just above the mouth of Pearl river was high and dry land affording a good place to land provided there were no rebels there. So, we concluded to land just above the mouth of Pearl river and remain there till morning so we rounded in and found a good camping ground and tied up. It will be observed that where there was a probability of danger we always tied up, otherwise we anchored. After placing our Enfields in a convient place and our navies nearby, we lay down to sleep, but we had not lain there long when on the acute ear of the soldiers came the sound of the distant tramp of troops marching, and on straining our ears we heard the steady tramp of the trained soldiers and we listened and peered in the darkness to determine what was coming, while nearer and nearer it came, yes we were in for it now, we were paroled prisoners and if taken, the pine trees along the shore, next day would be bearing full grown yankees, we in our imagination could see ourselves dangling from some pine tree amusing some rebel camp and there was but one way out of it now, we must try bluff and brass. So when this marching troop had reached a proper distance, we with a firm voice, cried out, Halt! Halt! or we will order the whole regiment to fire. Click, click, click, went the locks of our Enfields. They halted, surrender or we fire, we cried. "We surrender" a voice cried. Ground arms and move off to the right, we ordered, when down went their arms and they moved off a little ways, and we immediately conferred with them and found one 1st Luetenant and thirty two privates who had surrendered to a whole regiment, as they thought, which regiment consisted of but eight hoosiers.

Now we were in another predicament. There we were, eight union soldiers, two Louisana citizens and thirty-two rebel prisoners. It was with us again like it was with the Spanish vessel, we did not know what to do with them. To report to the command at Fort Pike was a difficult thing to do at this hour of the night and to remain here with all these prisoners till daylight should reveal our strength, was still more dangerous. So we placed four guards over our prisoners and reported to our imaginary regiment for orders, but this was only a ruse to enable us to hold a council of war, so we concluded to raise a lantern at our mast head as a flag of truce and take sixteen of the prisoners and row across to Ft. Pike, leaving the others there with the two citizens, still under guard. We gave first citizen pilot to understand that if he by word or deed should betray us, he would instantly receive a free pass to the "happy hunting grounds," and he understood this perfectly well, while our fisherman was perfectly honest and stood in with us. So we shoved off and rowed over, and while doing this we persuaded the rebels to lend us a helping hand, so on we went making the oars splash in the water in order to warn the guards at the Fort, and on coming to the outpost we were halted and we immediately informed the guard that we wanted to see the commanding officer and requested that one of us be sent to him at once, but he informed us that we could not see him until morning. We then requested that he call the corporal of the guard, which he did, and in due time that officer came and we stated the importance of our business and showed him our pass from Gen. Sherman and he at once consented to take one of us to the commandant's quarters, so we went and aroused the commander and exhibited to him our papers and gave a full explanation of affairs when he at once received the prisoners we had brought over and sent some soldiers back with us to receive the others and by the time we had done all this the dawn of morning was upon us and a night's sleep and rest gone, but this we did not mind since we had escaped a rebel noose through brass and bluff, and after passing through the night's toil and excitement we were glad to accept the beautiful calm bright morning and since our mission was ended we had nothing to do except sail up through Lake Ponchartrain—the nearest route to the city—and report but it was so calm that we were compelled to lay here until late in the evening awaiting a breeze to move our craft, during this time we had a good time visiting Fort Pike and telling stories and joking our old fisherman about shooting that porpoise and the storm he had predicted would overtake us, which prediction he still adhered too in the face of such fine weather as it now was. Along about an hour by sun, we concluded, in order to be doing something, to get aboard and lazily row up through the narrows by Lake Pike into Lake Ponchartrain and finding this very laborious we went very slowly up to, and passing by the great guns commanding the straights; but we kept on until we reached the waters of the Lake by which time the sun had gone down behind the western waters and the evening was beautiful and pleasant, and just now a slight breeze sprang up, and to lure us on, a beautiful island made its appearance some few miles up the lake (whether this was a myth or mirage the writer never knew, having passed there frequently since but never could find that island) and we at once determined to sail up to this beautiful island and camp for the night, so we head and move that way slowly when soon the breeze began to increase and darkness soon hovered about us and shut off our view of the island and suddenly the fliting clouds began to overspread the sky, and the wind began rolling the sea up in great foamy waves, just then we heard our fisherman murmer something about that porpose, but we had no time now to listen to superstition. The clouds grew thicker and heavier, and the darkness became intense; the wind was now moaning through our rigging, while the waves about us were slashing, splashing and raging with angry threatnings, while the sails of our little bark was now dipping the waves, now on thie side then on that, and under the direction of our fisherman we had trimmed our vessel for a storm which was now raging in all its fury. Where is our island? And why could we not reach it? Our ship reared and plunged while our sails almost drowning us with their foamy drippings, as they swung from side to side; our light was blown out and our compass was of no avail in such a storm and here we were, in total darkness, in the midst of a raging storm; with rebels on our right and sharks in our rear and about us, and the maddened waves threatening to swallow us up while the winds were singing a mournful requiem. We had evidently missed the island, and there was nothing but the broad expanse of raging waters on every hand; hope now seemed gone; but three of us able for duty while others were down in the hold making peace with their Maker in various tones of despairing prayer, as solemn as in the visible presence of Almighty God. Some of these prayers, now the danger is all over, seem a little laughable, and we can not now refrain from giving one of them as now remembered and copied from an old letter written soon after the occurence, viz: "Oh, Lord! I have stolen a little; I have lied a little; been a bad boy, and cursed a little; but Oh, Lord, I meant no harm by it. At that time how awful! How solemn! But now a little funny. The storm still raged; every gust of wind, every wave, and every plunge of the vessel seemed to threaten instant death as hour after hour we still sped on and on, we knew not where, till finally we ran up near an island just in our front. Columbus and his crew could not have been more rejoiced on their discovery of the New World, than we were on this occasion. We had presence of mind enough not to run boldly upon this land but ventured round to the leeward of the island which broke the force of the waves and there we anchored at about 3 o'clock in the morning, and like a parsel of wet rats we lay down to rest till morning, which soon came, beautiful and bright; the winds and waves had spent their force and there was nothing to indicate that there had been a storm but the great swells that were now quietly rolling and settling down into a peaceful calm; the sky was clear and the sun rose right in the north, pretty warm, and after resting awhile—for our nerves were yet unsteady—we made our reckoning and started on our journey for Lake End in the rear of New Orleans, and with fair sailing we made our destination late in the evening; reported to headquarters; made our return of Liza Jane, rigging, and the chart we had attempted to make, and were discharged.

Engagements From '62 to '65, 67th Ind. Vols.

Murfordsville, Ky., Sept. 14 to 17, '62.
Chickasaw Bayou, Miss., Dec. 29 to 31st, '62.
Arkansas Post, Ark., Jan. 11, '63.
Bombardment of Grand Gulf, Miss., April 20, '63.
Port Gibson, Miss., May 1, '63.
Raymond, Miss., May 12, '63.
Champion Hill, Miss., May 16, '63.
Big Black River Bridge, Miss., May 17, '63.
Seige and capture of Vicksburg, Miss., May 18 to July 14, '63.
Jackson, Miss., seige and capture, July 10 to 17, '63.
Opelousas, La., Oct. 21, '63.
Grand Coteau, La., Nov. 3, '63.
Matagorda Bay, Texas, Dec. 29 and 30, '63.
Grand Ecore, La., April 3, '64.
Saline Cross Roads, La., April 8, '64.
Mansfield, La., April 9, '64.
Cane River Crossing, La., April 23, '64.
Cane River, La., April 24, '64.
Alexandria, La., April 26, '64.
Hunt's Plantation, La., May 1, '64.
Dun's Bayou, La., May 5, '64.
Bayou De Lamora, La., May 12, '64.
Avayelles Prairie, La., May 13, '64.
Yellow Bayou, La., May 18, '64.
Old River, La., June 5th, '64.
Anhupaloga Bayou, La., Nov. 25 to Dec. 5, '64.
Fort Cains, Ala., Aug. 2 to 5, '64.
Fort Morgan, Ala., Aug. 5 to 23, '64.
Pollard, Ala., March 25, '65.
Fort Blakely, Ala., seige and capture, April 2 to 9, '65.

FIELD OFFICERS OF THE SIXTY-SEVENTH REGIMENT INDIANA VOLUNTEERS.

NAME AND RANK.	RESIDENCE.	DATE OF COM.	DATE OF MUSTER.	REMARKS.
Colonel				
Frank Emerson.	Brownstown.	August 22, '62	August 22, '62	Disability of wounds. Discharged Sept. 30, 1864.
Lieut. Cols.				
Theodore A. Bushler.	Bedford.	August 22, '62	August 22, '62	Dismissed from service for disobeying orders, March 15, '64.
Francis A. Sears.	"	March 16, '64	January 3, '65.	Transferred to 24th Ind as Lieut C
Majors				
Augustus A. Abolett.	Columbus.	Sept. 5th, '62	Sept. 5th, '62.	Killed at Mumf'de, Ky. Sep 14 62
Francis A. Sears.	Bedford.	Dec. 1st, '62	Dec. 3rd, '62.	Promoted to Lieut Col.
Adjutant				
George W. Richardson.	Madison.	Aug. 25th, '62	August 29th, '62	Tranf'd to 24th Ind, as 1st Lieut Co. 1. Dec 10, '64.
Quartermaster				
Joseph B. Newcomb.	Vernon.	July 19th, '62	July 19th, '62.	Resigned July 26, '63.
Merrit A. Read.	"	July 28th, '63	Dec. 11th, '63.	Mustered out on consolidation.
Chaplains				
Stephen Bowers.	Brownstown.	Sept. 1st, '62	Sept. 1st, '62.	Resigned May 4th, '63.
Lyman Schittenden.	"	Sept. 18th, '63	Sept. 25th, '63.	Transferred to 24th Ind.
Surgeons				
Jonas W. Gerrish.	Paris.	Aug. 22, '62	August 22d, '62.	Resigned August 13, '63.
Charles S. Boynton.	Hope.	March 5, '64	April 17th, '64.	Transferred to 24th Ind.
Assistant Surgeons				
James W. F. Gerrish.	Paris.	July 29th, '62	July 29th, '62.	Promoted Surgeon
" Dodd.	Harrodsburg.	Oct. 22nd, '62	October 22d, '62.	Resigned April 14, '63.
" Bryan.	Bloomington	Dec. 6th, '62	Dec. 6th, '62.	Resigned May 27, '63.
" A Burton.	Mitchell.	May 29th, '63	May 29th, '63.	Transferred to 24th Ind.

LIST OF MUSICAL STAFF SIXTY SEVENTH REGIMENT INDIANA VOLUNTEERS.

NAME.	MUSTERED 1862.	REMARKS.
Honrow Blackburn,	August 19th.	Promoted to fife Sept. 1, '62, mustered out July 19, '65
Chang White,	" "	Promoted drum maj. Sept 1, mustered out Nov.
Andrew McPike,	" "	Discharged for disability.
Richard W Ryan,	" "	
John W. Himes,	" "	
William Luch,	" "	
Benjamin Platt,	" "	
James Scott,	" "	
George W. Parker,	" "	Mustered out July 16th, '65.
Oliver M. Glasson,	" "	" " 19th. "
James Combs,	20th	
William B. Hart,	19th	Promoted drum maj Dec 9, '62, mustered out July '65
William C. Sampson,	" "	
Benjamin F. Aiken,	20th	Mustered out July 19, '65.
George W. Bruner,	" "	" " "
Isaac Johnson,	" "	" " "
Francis M. Lucknow,	" "	" " "

INDIANA VOLUNTEERS.

SIXTY-SEVENTH REGIMENT—THREE YEARS SERVICE.

ENLISTED MEN OF COMPANY "A."

Name and Rank.	Residence.	Date of Muster. 1862.	Remarks.
First Sergeant.			
Mitchell, David T............	....	Aug. 16......	Promoted 2d Lieutenant.
Sergeants.			
Anderson, James L...........	....	Aug. 19......	Discharged May 26, '65; disability
McCain, James H............	....	Aug. 19......	
McCain, Washington C......	....	Aug. 19......	
Baily, John S.................	....	Aug. 19......	Mustered out July 19, '65, as 1st Sergeant.
Corporals.			
Gyger, Isaiah..................	....	Aug. 19......	
Harrell, William J............	....	Aug. 19......	Mustered out July 19, '65, as Sergeant.
Johnson, William S..........	....	Aug. 19......	Mustered out July 19, '65, as private.
Eldridge, William N.........	....	Aug. 19......	Killed at Munfordsville, Ky., Sept. 14, '62.
Stoessel, Charles............	....	Aug. 19......	
Scott, Reuben B..............	....	Aug. 19......	Mustered out July 19, '65.
Anderson, Charles T.........	....	Aug. 19......	
Day, Samuel L...............	....	Aug. 19......	
Musicians.			
Blckburn, Monroe............	....	Aug. 19......	Mustered out July 19, '65.
White, Chancey..............	....	Aug. 19......	
Privates.			
Adams, James................	....	Aug. 19......	Mustered out July 19, '65.
Allen, Joseph.................	....	Aug. 19......	
Accom, Henry J.............	....	Aug. 19......	Mustered out July 19, '65.
Beavers, George W..........	....	Aug. 19......	
Besbig, August...............	....	Aug. 19......	
Bird, Samuel..................	....	Aug. 19......	
Bossert, Jacob................	....	Aug. 19......	Mustered out July 19, '64.
Bowman, James..............	....	Aug. 19......	
Bowman, William............	....	Aug. 19......	
Bowman, Isaac D............	....	Aug. 19......	
Brackenridge, Thos. W.....	....	Aug. 19......	
Brdiwell, Carter..............	....	Aug. 19......	Mustered out July 19, '63.
Bridwell, Alfred..............	....	Aug. 19......	
Bringer, George M...........	....	Aug. 19......	
Brown, William H............	....	Aug. 19......	Mustered out July 19, '65, as Sergeant.
Brown, Robert F.............	....	Aug. 19......	
Crawford, Daniel............	....	Aug. 19......	
Chestnut, Thomas J.........	....	Aug. 19......	
Cooper, Daniel B.............	....	Aug. 19......	Mustered out July 19, '65.
Dale, Eli M....................	....	Aug. 19......	
Darnell, Alvanian............	....	Aug. 19......	
Davis, Henry P...............	....	Aug. 19......	Transferred to 24th Regiment July 13, '64.
Davis, Charles................	....	Aug. 19......	
Day, Jesse J..................	....	Aug. 19......	Mustered out July 19, '65.
Denney, William.............	....	Aug. 19......	Discharged May 23, '65; disability.
Dooks, James M.............	....	Aug. 19......	Mustered out July 19, '65.
Dougherty, Hugh............	....	Aug. 19......	
Emery, George D............	....	Aug. 19......	
Etchison, Jesse...............	....	Aug. 19......	
Fields, Pleasant..............	....	Aug. 19......	
Fisher, William M...........	....	Aug. 19......	
Frankle, Joseph..............	....	Aug. 19......	
Frost, James..................	....	Aug. 19......	
Garrity, Thomas.............	....	Aug. 19......	Mustered out July 19, '65.
Gerrison, John C............	....	Aug. 19......	
Giles, Chrispon D...........	....	Aug. 19......	Mustered out July 19, '65.
Haverly, Frederick..........	....	Aug. 19......	
Huff, James...................	....	Aug. 19......	
Huston, James E............	....	Aug. 19......	Mustered out July 19, '65, as Corporal.
Johnson, John................	....	Aug. 19......	
Johnson, William C.........	....	Aug. 19......	
Kaustenbader, Charles.....	....	Aug. 19......	Mustered out July 19, '65.

SIXTY-SEVENTH REGIMENT INFANTRY

Name and Rank.	Residence.	Date of Muster, 1862.	Remarks.
Keener, John B		Aug. 19	Mustered out July 19, '65.
Keithly, Jesse W		Aug. 19	" " "
Kelly, Francis J		Aug. 19	
Lamb, Edward		Aug. 19	
Lamb, Josiah		Aug. 19	
Lewis, Nelson		Aug. 19	
Long, William		Aug. 19	
Lats, Otto		Aug. 19	
Lovell, Shelton S		Aug. 19	
Lynn, John N		Aug. 19	
Malott, Henry C		Aug. 19	Mustered out July 19, '65.
Malott, John		Aug. 19	
McLellen, Samuel		Aug. 19	
McWilliams, Ingo D		Aug. 19	
Nunnally, John H		Aug. 19	Mustered out July 19, '65.
Odell, Tobias M		Aug. 19	
Pace, Hardy		Aug. 19	
Payne, William		Aug. 19	
Payne, Jacob		Aug. 19	Mustered out July 19, '65.
Perkins, John		Aug. 19	
Philips, David		Aug. 19	
Rariden, Zimri F		Aug. 19	
Sears, James M		Aug. 19	
Sears, Rainy		Aug. 19	
Scrutchfield, H. F		Aug. 19	Mustered out July 19, '65.
Shenille, Rable W		Aug. 19	Mustered out June 6, '65.
Sipes, Pleasant		Aug. 19	
Smith, Jacob		Aug. 19	Promoted 2d Lieutenant.
Smith, Edwin L		Aug. 19	
Tannehill, Hugh H		Aug. 19	
Tannehill, James S		Aug. 19	Mustered out July 19, '65.
Terrell, Robert		Aug. 19	
Turney, Joseph		Aug. 19	
Turney, John T		Aug. 19	
Turner, James M		Aug. 19	Mustered out July 19, '65.
Whitted, James M		Aug. 19	
Young, Lewis R		Aug. 19	Mustered out July 19, '65.
Recruits.			
Anderson, Joseph M		Nov. 22, '64	Transferred to Co. "A," 24th Regt., July 13, '65.
Johnson, John		Nov. 11, '64	" " " "
Ramsey, George M		Nov. 18, '64	" " " "

ENLISTED MEN OF COMPANY "B."

Name and Rank.	Residence.	Date of Muster, 1862.	Remarks.
First Sergeant.			
Buskirk, William H	Bloomington	Aug. 19	Promoted 2d Lieutenant.
Sergeants.			
Gentry, James W		Aug. 19	Promoted 1st Lieutenant.
Hubbard, David W		Aug. 19	Mustered out Supernumerary.
Wilson, Thomas J		Aug. 19	Mustered out June 6, '65
Rollins, Daniel S		Aug. 19	
Corporals.			
Malcim, Francis M		Aug. 19	
Stepp, George L		Aug. 19	Mustered out July 19, '65.
Gillaspy, John J		Aug. 19	
Staly, William		Aug. 19	
Lafavors, Jacob C		Aug. 19	Mustered out June 6, '65.
Anderson, Andrew D		Aug. 19	
Bartin, John E		Aug. 19	Mustered out July 19, '65.
Hill, Julius A		Aug. 19	" " "
Musicians.			
McPike, Andrew J		Aug. 19	
Ryan, Robert W		Aug. 19	
Wagoner.			
Adams, William R		Aug. 19	
Privates.			
Anderson, John E		Aug. 19	Mustered out July 19, '65.
Ashbaugh, William		Aug. 19	

INDIANA VOLUNTEERS.

Name and Rank.	Residence.	Date of Muster. 1862.	Remarks.
Bastin, Jonathan H		Aug. 19	Mustered out June 30, '65.
Bastin, Jeremiah O		Aug. 19	Died at Grand Gulf, Miss., May, '63.
Bastin, Thomas B		Aug. 19	
Baugh, Henry		Aug. 19	
Baugh, Levi H		Aug. 19	
Baugh, Abner		Aug. 19	
Baugh, Ephraim		Aug. 19	
Bowman, Benjamin C		Aug. 19	Mustered out July 19, '65.
Bowlin, Christopher		Aug. 19	
Bowlin, Bolum		Aug. 19	
Brown, George M		Aug. 19	
Burpo, John T		Aug. 19	
Carr, William		Aug. 19	Mustered out July 19, '65.
Craiger, Isaiah		Aug. 19	" " "
Daggy, George W		Aug. 19	" " "
Denney, Samuel jr		Aug. 19	" " "
Denney, William		Aug. 19	
Elliott, Stephen B		Aug. 19	Mustered out July 19, '65.
Fulford, Jonathan H		Aug. 19	" " "
Fulford, Thomas F		Aug. 19	
Fulford, James J		Aug. 19	
Gentry, William B		Aug. 19	Discharged Jan. 7, '65; disability.
Gaskins, Joseph F		Aug. 19	
Gaskins, Isaac S		Aug. 19	
Gaskins, Samuel		Aug. 19	
Gilopy, John S		Aug. 19	
Graham, George W		Aug. 19	
Hill, Gaston M		Aug. 19	
Hollar, Israel		Aug. 19	
Helton, Adam		Aug. 19	Mustered out June 20, '65.
Helton, William H		Aug. 19	
Hancock, Greenberry W		Aug. 19	Discharged Jan. 7, '65; disability.
Hite, William W		Aug. 19	Mustered out July 19, '65.
Hurley, Miles W		Aug. 19	
Hocker, Mahlon		Aug. 19	
Hasket, Daniel		Aug. 19	
Hasket, John		Aug. 19	
Jax, James N		Aug. 19	
Kindrick, Dennis C		Aug. 19	
Lafavers, Isaac J		Aug. 19	Mustered out July 19, '62.
Milans, Noah C		Aug. 19	
McNamara, Edward J		Aug. 19	Mustered out July 19, '62.
McMerris, Benjamin S		Aug. 19	
McManis, John T		Aug. 19	Mustered out July 19, '62.
McHenry, Joseph H		Aug. 19	" " "
Mosier, Jeremiah		Aug. 19	" " "
Murphy, Jeremiah		Aug. 19	
McComic, George		Aug. 19	
Neal, George W		Aug. 19	
Neal, Marion		Aug. 19	
Patterson, John E		Aug. 19	Mustered out July 19, '65.
Payne, Isaiah		Aug. 19	
Pryor, Isaac		Aug. 19	Mustered out July 19, '65.
Robinson, James W		Aug. 19	
Rar, John J		Aug. 19	
Riddle, William		Aug. 19	
Richardson, Jonathan		Aug. 19	
Smith, William		Aug. 19	Mustered out July 19, '65.
Smith, David F		Aug. 19	
Smith, John		Aug. 19	Mustered out July 19, '65.
Smith, John P		Aug. 19	
Stepp, Joshua		Aug. 19	Mustered out July 19, '62.
Stepp, Francis M		Aug. 19	
South, William		Aug. 19	
Summit, Joel B		Aug. 19	Mustered out July 19, '65.
Stephenson, Francis M		Aug. 19	" " "
Sims, James E		Aug. 19	[out June 20, '65.
Sims, Robert		Aug. 19	Transferred to V. R. C., April 29, '65; must'd
Stine, John		Aug. 19	
Switzer, Samuel		Aug. 19	
Simmons, James		Aug. 19	Mustered out July 19, '65.
Thomas, James B		Aug. 19	" " "
Thomas, John H		Aug. 19	
Turner, James		Aug. 19	
Taylor, Montgomery		Aug. 19	Mustered out July 19, '65;
Woodall, Benjamin F		Aug. 19	Died at St. Louis, April, '64.
Wise, Tighlman H		Aug. 19	Mustered out July 19, '65
Williams, Mathias		Aug. 19	" " "
York, William H		Aug. 19	Mustered out July 19, '65, as Corporal.

SIXTY-SEVENTH REGIMENT INFANTRY

ENLISTED MEN OF COMPANY "C."

Name and Rank.	Residence.	Date of Muster. 1862.	Remarks.
First Sergeant.			
Graham, William P.		Aug. 19	Transf'd to V. R. C. Dec. 24, '64, as private.
Sergeants.			
Hinds, James H.		Aug. 19	
Weyer, Edward P.		Aug. 19	
Wright, Marion		Aug. 19	Mustered out July 19, '65, as private.
Gale, Aurelius L.		Aug. 19	
Corporals.			
Richardson, George W.		Aug. 19	
Gale, Stephen B.		Aug. 19	
Spear, James W.		Aug. 19	Mustered out May 24, '65.
Woodard, Albert G.		Aug. 19	Mustered out July 19, '65.
Sale, John W.		Aug. 19	Promoted 2d Lieutenant.
Miller, William H. H.		Aug. 19	Mustered out July 19, '65.
Dewey, James B.		Aug. 19	" " "
Mathews, John C.		Aug. 19	
Musicians.			
Hinds, John W.		Aug. 19	
Luck, William		Aug. 19	
Wagoner.			
Temples, Ephraim J.		Aug. 19	
Privates.			
Adams, Andrew		Aug. 19	Mustered out July 19, '65.
Allison, James		Aug. 19	" " "
Ashby, William		Aug. 19	
Beers, Robert M.		Aug. 19	Mustered out July 19, '65, as Sergeant.
Boicourt, Thomas Jr.		Aug. 19	
Bolen, Simeon B.		Aug. 19	Mustered out July 19, '65.
Butler, Patrick		Aug. 19	" " "
Brooks, John W.		Aug. 19	
Brooks, Humphrey		Aug. 19	Mustered out July 19, '65.
Byfield, Vincent D.		Aug. 19	" " "
Cope, George W.		Aug. 19	
Chamberlain, Charles		Aug. 19	
Child, John A.		Aug. 19	
Crandell, Melville O.		Aug. 19	Mustered out July 19, '64.
Daily, Melvin E.		Aug. 19	" " "
Dunn, William M. Jr.		Aug. 19	
Dubach, George W.		Aug. 19	
Dreier, Henry Jr.		Aug. 19	
Elms, Rosington		Aug. 19	
Fox, George W.		Aug. 19	
Freeman, Harry		Aug. 19	
Goble, Jacob		Aug. 19	Mustered out July 19, '64.
Gohr, Peter		Aug. 19	
Green, Joseph A.		Aug. 19	
Glenn, Thomas		Aug. 19	
Graham, James G.		Aug. 16	
Heid, Michael G.		Aug. 19	
Hendricks, Thomas		Aug. 19	
Hinton, William T.		Aug. 19	
Hibben, Omar T.		Aug. 19	Mustered out July 19, '65.
Hinds, Rufus W.		Aug. 19	
Holmes, Robert		Aug. 19	
Holmes, Samuel L.		Aug. 19	
Holtzner, Charles		Aug. 19	Mustered out June 29, '65.
Jones, Casefus M.		Aug. 19	Mustered out July 19, '65.
Joyce, Smith		Aug. 19	
Kyle, John W.		Aug. 19	Mustered out July 19, '65.
Lathrop, Henry A.		Aug. 19	
Lane, William E.		Aug. 19	Mustered out July 19, '65, as 1st Sergeant.
Littecer, Henry J.		Aug. 19	
Lodge, Caleb		Aug. 19	
Lowe, John T.		Aug. 19	Mustered out July 19, '65.
Meier, Joseph		Aug. 19	" " "
Miller, John A.		Aug. 19	
Millsur, Jacob		Aug. 19	Mustered out July 19, '65.
Millin, Patrick		Aug. 19	" " "
Mitchell, James H.		Aug. 19	
Morrow, Robert		Aug. 19	Mustered out July 19, '65.
Monfort, John M.		Aug. 19	
McClure, David		Aug. 19	
McClelland, James E.		Aug. 19	Mustered out May 3, '65.

INDIANA VOLUNTEERS.

NAME AND RANK.	Residence.	Date of Muster. 1862.	REMARKS.
McGee, Robert A		Aug. 19	Mustered out July 19, '65.
McKay, Thomas H		Aug. 19	" " "
McMillan, William A		Aug. 19	" " "
Nodler, Peter		Aug. 19	
Quigley, William A		Aug. 19	Mustered out July 19, '65.
Reed, George W		Aug. 19	
Rea, George H		Aug. 19	
Repp, Valentine		Aug. 19	
Rogers, David W		Aug. 19	
Read, Merrit		Aug. 19	
Sampson, Henry C		Aug. 19	Mustered out July 19, '65.
Simms, Elijah		Aug. 19	" " "
Smith, Abner C		Aug. 19	
Smith, Patrick		Aug. 19	Mustered out July 19, '65.
Stratton, William D		Aug. 19	
Taylor, Oliver P		Aug. 19	
Temperly, William T		Aug. 19	Mustered out July 19, '65, as Corporal.
Tevis, Melancthron		Aug. 19	
Thomas, Jacob		Aug. 19	Mustered out June 30, '65.
Thompson, Napoleon W		Aug. 19	Mustered out July 19, '65.
Treadway, George		Aug. 19	Discharged, Feb. 13, '65; disability.
Ulmer, John		Aug. 19	Mustered out July 19, '65, as Corporal.
Weber, John A		Aug. 19	
Weber, Peter		Aug. 19	
Wilson, Joseph		Aug. 19	
Wilson, James B		Aug. 19	Mustered out July 19, '65.
Woodard, Willis I		Aug. 19	" " "
Woodard, Charles		Aug. 19	
Wright, George T		Aug. 19	
Young, William		Aug. 19	Mustered out July 19, '65, as Sergeant.
Young, James W		Aug. 19	
Recruits.			
Clegg, Henry		Jan. 7, '64	Transferred 24th Reg't, July 13, '65.
Clegg, Thomas		Jan. 7, '64	" " "
Divine, Isaac		Nov. 21, '64	" " "
Morton, Thomas C		Jan. 7, '64	" " "
Osgood, Merrill T		Jan. 7, '64	" " "
Yawter, Thomas S		Jan. 4, '64	" " "

ENLISTED MEN OF COMPANY "D."

NAME AND RANK.	Residence.	Date of Muster. 1862.	REMARKS.
First Sergeant.			
Abbett, Francis M		Aug. 19	
Sergeants.			
Brown, Horace L		Aug. 19	Promoted 2d Lieutenant.
Cavanaugh, William H		Aug. 19	
Loyd, William I		Aug. 19	
Bennett, Frank		Aug. 19	
Corporals.			
Cooper, Benjamin W		Aug. 19	
Mitchell, James E		Aug. 19	Mustered out June 20, '65, as Sergeant.
Cavanaugh, James		Aug. 19	
Baker, Joseph		Aug. 19	Mustered out July 19, '65.
Thompson, John W		Aug. 19	Mustered out May 12, '65.
Jones, Jasper, A		Aug. 19	
Cooace, George H		Aug. 19	Mustered out July 19, '65.
Smith, David		Aug. 19	
Musicians.			
Platt, Benjamin		Aug. 19	
Scott, James		Aug. 19	
Wagoner.			
Holmes, Benjamin B		Aug. 19	
Privates.			
Abbett, William A		Aug. 19	Mustered out July 19, '65, as Corporal.
Allen, Stephen D		Aug. 19	
Baker, David		Aug. 19	
Burns, William		Aug. 19	Mustered out July 19, '65.
Barkalow, John S		Aug. 19	" " "
Black, John C		Aug. 19	

Name and Rank.	Residence.	Date of Muster, 1862.	Remarks.
Brinkly, Jesse F.		Aug. 19	Mustered out July 19, '65.
Brown, Cullen		Aug. 19	
Bradbury, ——		Aug. 19	
Cady, Sanford C.		Aug. 19	Mustered out July 19, '65.
Cantrell, John W.		Aug. 19	" " "
Carter, George W.		Aug. 19	" " "
Cook, William L.		Aug. 19	" " "
Cutsinger, William		Aug. 19	
Collins, John W.		Aug. 19	
Cox, Ezra		Aug. 19	
Draper, Eli		Aug. 19	Mustered out July 19, '65.
Davis, Randall		Aug. 19	
Davis, William		Aug. 19	
Eth, John		Aug. 19	
Everoad, William		Aug. 19	Mustered out July 19, '65.
Fairall, John W.		Aug. 19	
Franklin, John M.		Aug. 19	Mustered out July 19, '65.
Fisher, John		Aug. 19	Discharged Jan. 12, '65; disability.
Green, Allen		Aug. 19	
Graves, Albert H.		Aug. 19	
Gale, John F.		Aug. 19	
Harsin, William A. M.		Aug. 19	Mustered out July 19, '65.
Hutchins, Andrew J.		Aug. 19	
Hill, Asa W.		Aug. 19	
Jewell, Martin B.		Aug. 19	
Johnston, James W.		Aug. 19	Mustered out July 19, '65.
Kean, William H.		Aug. 19	
Lazzelle, James L.		Aug. 19	
Lazzelle, Uriah W.		Aug. 19	Mustered out July 19, '65.
Lazzelle, George W.		Aug. 19	" " "
Lazzelle, Noble J. W.		Aug. 19	Mustered out May 31, '65.
Lennon, John		Aug. 19	Mustered out July 19, '65.
Lennon, Charles		Aug. 19	" " "
Lucky, Willis		Aug. 19	Discharged Jan 4, '65; disability.
Martin, Randolph		Aug. 19	
McCombs, Charles		Aug. 19	
Merring, John N.		Aug. 19	Mustered out July 19, '65.
Murray, James		Aug. 19	" " "
Metcalf, William R.		Aug. 19	Mustered out July 19, '65, as Corporal.
McDaniel, Thomas		Aug. 19	
Norton, William A.		Aug. 19	
Near, Frederick		Aug. 19	
Nolan, Sampson P.		Aug. 19	
Newsom, John S.		Aug. 19	
Ogden, Noah		Aug. 19	
Parisho, James H.		Aug. 19	Mustered out July 19, '65.
Parisho, Gabriel		Aug. 19	" " "
Poland, James		Aug. 19	
Poland, William F. M.		Aug. 19	Mustered out July 19, '65.
Puffenberger, Hezekiah		Aug. 19	
Riker, Samuel		Aug. 19	
Roberts, William H.		Aug. 19	Mustered out July 19, '65.
Ruthford, Jesse		Aug. 19	" " "
Scott, Philip W.		Aug. 19	
Silles, Harper		Aug. 19	
Sims, John D.		Aug. 19	
Shields, Abel F.		Aug. 19	
Sprague, James W.		Aug. 19	Mustered out July 19, '65, as Corporal.
Sprague, John W.		Aug. 19	" " "
Stont, George W.		Aug. 19	
Shafer, Enos		Aug. 19	
Snider, Levi		Aug. 19	Mustered out July 19, '65.
Stultz, John		Aug. 19	" " "
Shumway, Oscar		Aug. 19	Mustered out July 19, '65, as Sergeant.
Swingle, Simon P.		Aug. 19	
Taylor, Hiram		Aug. 19	Mustered out July 19, '65.
Taylor, James C.		Aug. 19	
Tilton, David R.		Aug. 19	Mustered out July 19, '65.
Thompson, Greenberry		Aug. 19	" " "
Thompson, Vincent		Aug. 19	
Thompson, Samuel R.		Aug. 19	
Wood, Henry		Aug. 19	
Walters, Thomas		Aug. 19	Mustered out July 19, '65.
Winland, Isaac		Aug. 19	
Whipple, John		Aug. 19	
Ward, Stephen G.		Aug. 19	
Recruits.			
Frothingham, William		Jan. 29, '64	Tranef'd to Co. "E," 24th Reg't, July 13, '65
Hauser, George		Jan. 27, '64	" " " "
Romine, Elijah		Jan. 28, '64	" " " "

INDIANA VOLUNTEERS.

ENLISTED MEN OF COMPANY "E."

Name and Rank.	Residence.	Date of Muster. 1862.	Remarks.
First Sergeant.			
Edmunds, Meredith R		Aug. 20	Promoted 2d Lieutenant.
Sergeants.			
Rodman, Thomas J		Aug. 20	Discharged, Jan. 13, '65; disability; 1st Serg't.
McCrary, James E		Aug. 20	
Tomson, John B		Aug. 20	
Wilson, John A		Aug. 20	Mustered out July 19, '65.
Corporals.			
Henderson, John T		Aug. 20	Discharged May 23, '65; disability; 1st Serg't.
Tucker, William P		Aug. 20	
Bohall, James		Aug. 20	Discharged Jan. 13, '65; disability.
Clayton, Archibald N		Aug. 20	
Baughman, Isaac N		Aug. 20	Mustered out July 19, '65, as Sergeant.
Umphries, George T		Aug. 20	
Ramey, Pleasant S		Aug. 20	
Stilwell, Charles W		Aug. 20	
Privates.			
Anderson, James		Aug. 20	
Atkins, James R		Aug. 20	
Ayers, Samuel		Aug. 20	
Ayers, William		Aug. 20	
Banks, George W		Aug. 20	
Bertwinger, Godfried		Aug. 20	Mustered out July 19, '65.
Blackater, George W		Aug. 20	
Bower, James V		Aug. 20	
Bosley, James		Aug. 20	Mustered out July 19, '65.
Burk, Harvey		Aug. 20	
Burt, Henry		Aug. 20	Discharged April 17, '65; disability.
Burrell, Reuben		Aug. 20	
Calaway, Chester		Aug. 20	Deserted May 29, '65.
Cash, George		Aug. 20	
Crabb, Marion		Aug. 20	Mustered out July 19, '65.
Croucher, William F		Aug. 20	" " "
Dobson, Henry W		Aug. 20	
Early, Sylvester H		Aug. 20	
Egg, Christian		Aug. 20	
Edkins, John		Aug. 20	
Emmons, Richard		Aug. 20	
England, James		Aug. 20	Mustered out July 19, '65.
England, John W		Aug. 20	
Ewing, James		Aug. 20	
Fordyce, William		Aug. 20	
Gossman, John O		Aug. 20	Mustered out July 19, '65, as Corporal.
Goen, Henry B		Aug. 20	Mustered out July 19, '65.
Gwen, James W		Aug. 20	
Gobble, Napoleon		Aug. 20	Mustered out July 19, '65.
Grimes, Theodore		Aug. 20	" " "
Grimes, William J		Aug. 20	
Hamilton, William W		Aug. 20	
Hartling, Charles		Aug. 20	Mustered out July 19, '65.
Hasler, Frederick		Aug. 20	" " "
Haney, William		Aug. 20	Mustered out July 19, '65, as Corporal.
Haney, Leonard		Aug. 20	
Holeman, William F		Aug. 20	Mustered out July 19, '65.
House, William		Aug. 20	
Ireland, George W		Aug. 20	
Ireland, Jonathan		Aug. 20	Mustered out July 19, '65.
Jarvis, Solomon		Aug. 20	
Johnson, James A		Aug. 20	
Johnson, William		Aug. 20	Killed on picket at Ft. Blakely, Ala., Apr. 5, '65
Johnson, Stephen B		Aug. 20	
Johnson, Elisha G		Aug. 20	
Johnson, George M		Aug. 20	
Johnson, John		Aug. 20	
Julian, George W		Aug. 20	
Kinworthy, John		Aug. 20	Mustered out July 19, '65.
Lewis, Thomas P		Aug. 20	" " "
Lenox, Moses		Aug. 20	
Martin, Terrel		Aug. 20	Mustered out July 19, '65.
Mattock, Hiram		Aug. 20	
McCrary, John W		Aug. 20	
McPherson, Henry C		Aug. 20	
McPherson, Joseph		Aug. 20	
Merritt, Andrew W		Aug. 20	Mustered out July 19, '65.
Mahanks, Fritz		Aug. 20	" " "

Name and Rank.	Residence.	Date of Muster. 1862.	Remarks.
Miller, Eli Warren		Aug. 20	
Mullis, Thomas		Aug. 20	
Nolde, Frank C.		Aug. 20	Mustered out July 19, '65.
Peters, John E.		Aug. 20	
Pearson, John M.		Aug. 20	Mustered out July 19, '65.
Reeves, Robert B.		Aug. 20	" " "
Rich, David		Aug. 20	"
Rich, Jonah		Aug. 20	
Richards, Joel W.		Aug. 20	Mustered out July 19, '65.
Rodman, James T.		Aug. 20	
Sanders, Thomas E.		Aug. 20	
Sabrooke, Thomas		Aug. 20	
Sewell, John C.		Aug. 20	Mustered out July 19, '65.
Shortridge, George W.		Aug. 20	
Skinner, George W.		Aug. 20	Mustered out July 19, '65, as Corporal.
Smith, James T.		Aug. 20	
Smith, Joseph L.		Aug. 20	Mustered out July 19, '65.
Spurgeon, Zachariah		Aug. 20	
Sutherland, Bluford		Aug. 20	Mustered out July 19, '65.
Taylor, James F.		Aug. 20	" " "
Thomas, Charles E.		Aug. 20	" " "
Tucker, James M.		Aug. 20	
Umphries, John W.		Aug. 20	
Watkins, John B.		Aug. 20	Mustered out July 19, '65.
Wheeler, William C.		Aug. 20	" " "
Wilkerson, Thomas J.		Aug. 20	
Wininger, Clemons		Aug. 20	

ENLISTED MEN OF COMPANY "F"

Name and Rank.	Residence.	Date of Muster. 1862.	Remarks.
First Sergeant.			
Peck, Lewis W.		Aug. 20	Promoted 1st Lieutenant.
Sergeants.			
Hinkley, Hugh G.		Aug. 20	
Walker, James		Aug. 20	
Murphy, John T.		Aug. 20	
Weddel, Jasper		Aug. 20	
Corporals.			
Scott, Alexander		Aug. 20	Mustered out July 19, '65.
Boem, John C.		Aug. 20	" " "
Byrne, Patrick H.		Aug. 20	Mustered out July 19, '65, as Sergeant.
Owen, John W.		Aug. 20	
Hughes, William T.		Aug. 20	Mustered out July 19, '65.
Sparks, Major A.		Aug. 20	
Louden, Jacob		Aug. 20	
Chambers, Elihu		Aug. 20	Mustered out July 19, '65.
Musician.			
Parker, George W.		Aug. 20	Mustered out July 16, '65.
Wagoner.			
Garrell, Josephus		Aug. 20	Mustered out July 19, '65.
Privates.			
Alexander, John S.		Aug. 20	Mustered out July 19, '65, as 1st Sergeant.
Barnett, David		Aug. 20	
Bound, David		Aug. 20	
Bottorf, Francis M.		Aug. 20	
Bowman, Henry		Aug. 20	
Bryon, John B.		Aug. 20	
Croutcher, William		Aug. 20	
Craig, Alamanzer C.		Aug. 20	Mustered out July 19, '65.
Croutcher, Green		Aug. 20	
Collins, George W.		Aug. 20	Deserted June 1, '64.
Dowling, William F.		Aug. 20	Mustered out May 31, '65.
Dowling, John H.		Aug. 20	Mustered out July 19, '65.
Duff, James P.		Aug. 20	
Dare, Collin		Aug. 20	
Davenport, Benjamin F.		Aug. 20	Mustered out July 19, '65.
Elliott, Martin F.		Aug. 20	Discharged March 19, '65, disability.
Evans, David B.		Aug. 20	
Etter, John W.		Aug. 20	

133

Name and Rank.	Residence.	Date of Muster 1862.	Remarks.
Etter, James		Aug. 20	
Fowler, Charles H		Aug. 20	
Fowler, John T		Aug. 20	Mustered out July 19, '65, as Corporal.
Goen, Hasten		Aug. 20	
Goen, George W		Aug. 20	Mustered out July 19, '65.
Gray, George B		Aug. 20	
Hoover, James		Aug. 20	
Hollowell, James		Aug. 20	
Huffington, Sylvester		Aug. 20	
Henderson, Aaron M		Aug. 20	Mustered out July 19, '65.
Hatfield, George D		Aug. 20	
Henderlider, John M		Aug. 20	Promoted 2d Lieutenant.
Hays, Andrew J		Aug. 20	
Meachem, William		Aug. 20	
Isaacks, Andrew J		Aug. 20	
Martin, Jacob G		Aug. 20	
Murphy, William A		Aug. 20	Mustered out July 19, '65.
McLary, John		Aug. 20	
Moosbow, Patrick		Aug. 20	Mustered out July 19, '65.
Mondon, Demerinh		Aug. 20	
Newby, Charles H		Aug. 20	
Pfint, John		Aug. 20	
Prior, Moses B		Aug. 20	
Russell, Kincheo		Aug. 20	
Reynolds, Charles L		Aug. 20	
Reynolds, John S		Aug. 20	Mustered out July 19, '65.
Reynolds, Michael		Aug. 20	Mustered out July 19, '65; Corporal.
Richards, James H		Aug. 20	Mustered out June , 8'65.
Reynolds, Jacob		Aug. 20	
Reed, Elisha		Aug. 20	
Reuben, Searcy		Aug. 20	
Smith, Alcana		Aug. 20	Mustered out July 19, '65.
Sparks, Stephen		Aug. 20	" " "
Soon, Alfred		Aug. 20	" " "
Sutton, Jacob H		Aug. 20	
Soos, James P		Aug. 20	
Searcy, Jeremiah		Aug. 20	
Sullivan, James T		Aug. 20	
Thompson, John F		Aug. 20	Mustered out July 19, '65.
Tatlock, Joseph		Aug. 20	
Tanner, Joseph L		Aug. 20	Mustered out July 19, '65.
Williams, John W		Aug. 20	
Weddell, Hamilton		Aug. 20	
Wloesinger, Adam		Aug. 20	Mustered out July 19, '65.
Weddel, John A		Aug. 20	" " "
Worlow, Joseph W		Aug. 20	" " "
Weddle, Andrew J		Aug. 20	" " "
Walker, Daniel P		Aug. 20	
Worlow, George H		Aug. 20	
Recruits			
Richards, John		Oct. 13, '63	Transferred 24th Reg't, July 13, '65.
Scott, John A		Oct. 15, '63	" " "
Waddle, Amos		Feb. 24, '64	" " "
Wright, Austin		Feb. 24, '64	" " "

ENLISTED MEN OF COMPANY "G."

Name and Rank.	Residence.	Date of Muster 1862.	Remarks.
First Sergeant.			
Sweany, Achilles		April 20	
Sergeants.			
Brooks, William M		April 20	Discharged Dec. 20, '64; disability; private.
Duckworth, Robert		April 20	
Bundy, William		April 20	
Smith, Jesse		April 20	Discharged Jan. 21, '65; disability.
Corporals.			
Duckworth, William		April 20	Discharged May 23, '63; disability.
Garrett, Austin		April 20	
Bartup, Jesse		April 20	Mustered out July 19, '65.
Sweany, Gordon		April 20	Mustered out July 19, '65, as private.
Clark, James L		April 20	
Parks, George W		April 20	Mustered out June 15, '65.

Name and Rank.	Residence.	Date of Muster. 1862.	Remarks.
Beadle, Isaiah		Aug. 20	Mustered out June 15, '65.
Ewan, Phineas		Aug. 20	Mustered out July 19, '65, as Sergeant.
Musicians.			
Gloesan, Oliver M		Aug. 20	Mustered out July 19, '65.
Comar, James		Aug. 20	
Wagoner.			
Abbett, Major A		Aug. 20	
Privates.			
Adams, Ebenezar		Aug. 20	
Beadle, John		Aug. 20	
Beadle, Luther		Aug. 20	Mustered out July 19, '65.
Burkdall, Stephen		Aug. 20	" " "
Boggs, Joshua		Aug. 20	
Bunton, William S		Aug. 20	Mustered out July 19, '65.
Bates, N. S		Aug. 20	Mustered out July 19, '65, as Sergeant.
Barnes, Abraham		Aug. 20	
Cox, Wilson		Aug. 20	Mustered out July 19, '65.
Crane, John M		Aug. 20	" " "
Crane, Chester Jr		Aug. 20	
Cordell, Howard		Aug. 20	Mustered out July 19, '65.
Crane, John F		Aug. 20	Transf'd to V. R. C.; must'd out July 25, '65.
Doan, George W		Aug. 20	
Dennison, Daniel W		Aug. 20	
Dennison, Edward		Aug. 20	
Dennison, George		Aug. 20	Mustered out July 19, '65.
Ewan, Isaac		Aug. 20	
Edwards, William		Aug. 20	
Easter, Solomon		Aug. 20	
Gossett, Joel		Aug. 20	Mustered out July 19, '65.
Gregory, Joseph		Aug. 20	
Gardner, Beecher		Aug. 20	Mustered out July 19, '65.
Gleason, Jasper		Aug. 20	" " "
Gross, Martin		Aug. 20	Mustered out June 26, '65.
Gossett, John W		Aug. 20	
Gerard, Martin		Aug. 20	Mustered out July 19, '65.
Gochnat, Charles		Aug. 20	" " "
Gilbert, Whitney		Aug. 20	" " "
Heltman, Lewis W. H		Aug. 20	" " "
Huntman, John H		Aug. 20	" " "
Hepler, Elza		Aug. 20	
Hooker, George D		Aug. 20	
Hane, William		Aug. 20	Discharged May 23, '65; disability.
Harding, John B		Aug. 20	
Harrison, Reuben		Aug. 20	
Jones, Nicholas		Aug. 20	Mustered out July 19, '65.
Johnston, James S		Aug. 20	Discharged Dec. 16, '64; disability.
Lewis, John Q. A		Aug. 20	
Myers, James		Aug. 20	
Matthews, Josiah		Aug. 20	
Mascher, Frederick G		Aug. 20	Mustered out July 19, '65.
Miller, Conrad		Aug. 20	
McCormick, John H		Aug. 20	Promoted 1st Lieutenant.
Newby, Nathan S		Aug. 20	
Noling, William H		Aug. 20	Mustered out July 19, '65.
Nowling, Newton		Aug. 20	
Olmstead, Samuel		Aug. 20	
Pfeffenberger, Joseph		Aug. 20	
Patrick, Andrew H		Aug. 20	Mustered out July 19, '65.
Ruddick, Edward		Aug. 20	" " "
Ruddick, Thomas J		Aug. 20	
Ruddick, Scott		Aug. 20	
Ruddick, Lindley		Aug. 20	Mustered out July 19, '65.
Ruddick, Silas		Aug. 20	" " "
Reed, Solomon		Aug. 20	
Rehmet, Thomas J		Aug. 20	
Strawther, Aaron A		Aug. 20	Mustered out July 19, '65.
Simpson, Alfred		Aug. 20	
Sweaney, Joshua M		Aug. 20	Mustered out July 19, '65.
Sweany, Alexander T		Aug. 20	" " "
Sweany, Jacob		Aug. 20	
Stewart, Jacob		Aug. 20	Mustered out July 19, '65.
Spear, Charles W		Aug. 20	" " "
Sweany, Jefferson		Aug. 20	
Smith, Jesse		Aug. 20	
Tonne, Henry		Aug. 20	Mustered out July 19, '65.
Thompson, John W		Aug. 20	" " "
Vaughn, Edgar E		Aug. 20	
Vaughn, William		Aug. 20	Mustered out June 19, '65.

Name and Rank.	Residence.	Date of Muster, 1862.	Remarks.
Wagner, John		Aug. 20	
Winslow, Jesse W		Aug. 20	Mustered out July 19, '65.
White, Joseph B		Aug. 20	
Whitson, John W		Aug. 20	
Williams, Edghill		Aug. 20	
Recruits.			
Crane, Jabez T		Nov. 3, '62	Transf'd to Co. "A," 24th Reg't, July 13, '65.
Rude, John J		Nov. 3, '62	" " " "
Turnbull, John C		Nov. 3, '62	" " " "

ENLISTED MEN OF COMPANY "H."

Name and Rank.	Residence.	Date of Muster, 1862.	Remarks.
First Sergeant.			
Stewart, John L		Aug. 19	Promoted 1st Lieutenant.
Sergeants.			
Lemon, Francis M		Aug. 19	
Morris, Wilson		Aug. 19	
Hostetler, Benjamin N		Aug. 19	Promoted 2d Lieutenant.
Burton, Eli		Aug. 19	Mustered out July 19, '65.
Corporals.			
Smart, Coleman D		Aug. 19	Mustered out July 19, '65, as Sergeant.
Warne, James P		Aug. 19	Transferred to 24th Reg't, as Q. M. Sergeant.
Moore, John		Aug. 19	
Wright, Varcienno		Aug. 19	
McIntire, William		Aug. 19	
Giles, William		Aug. 19	
Burton, Joseph A		Aug. 19	Mustered out July 19, '65.
Edwards, William H		Aug. 19	
Musicians.			
Hart, William H		Aug. 19	Mustered out July 19, '65.
Sampson, William C		Aug. 19	" " "
Wagoner.			
Price, William		Aug. 19	Mustered out July 19, '65.
Privates.			
Ash, Joseph		Aug. 19	
Beasley, Thomas		Aug. 19	Mustered out July 19, '65
Beasley, John		Aug. 19	" " "
Bosell, Stephen		Aug. 19	
Brown, William		Aug. 19	Mustered out July 8, '65.
Burton, David G		Aug. 19	
Burton, William A		Aug. 19	
Burton, Gordon		Aug. 19	
Burton, Riley D		Aug. 19	Mustered out May 22, '65.
Burton, Isam		Aug. 19	Mustered out July 19, '65.
Burton, Hugh H		Aug. 19	" " "
Bundy, Alexander		Aug. 19	
Bundy, Denton		Aug. 19	
Brewer, William M		Aug. 19	
Cox, William		Aug. 19	
Cox, Richard		Aug. 19	Mustered out July 19, '65.
Carpenter, William		Aug. 19	
Carpenday, Robert		Aug. 19	
Clark, Eli		Aug. 19	Mustered out July 19, '65.
Cleveland, Josiah		Aug. 19	" " "
Conley, Solomon		Aug. 19	
Conley, Franklin M		Aug. 19	
Cunningham, James L		Aug. 19	
Daws, Henry		Aug. 19	
Dewhurst, John		Aug. 19	
Edwards, Allen		Aug. 19	Mustered out July 19, '65.
Edwards, David B		Aug. 19	
Edwards, Alexander		Aug. 19	Mustered out July 19, '65.
Edwards, Eli O		Aug. 19	
Edwards, Wesley		Aug. 19	
Edwards, Allen		Aug. 19	
Fielder, Nelson S		Aug. 19	
Fielder, James T		Aug. 19	Mustered out July 19, '65.
Ford, John		Aug. 19	

Vol. VI.—6

Name and Rank.	Residence.	Date of Muster. 1862.	Remarks.
Gataway, William		Aug. 19	
Garges, William H		Aug. 19	Mustered out July 19, '65.
Giles, John C		Aug. 19	
Gross, Absalom		Aug. 19	Mustered out July 19, '65.
Grossclass, John		Aug. 19	Mustered out May 23, '65.
Hartley, William		Aug. 19	
Hartney, Joseph		Aug. 19	
Hamilton, John B		Aug. 19	
Hardman, Peter		Aug. 19	Mustered out July 19, '65, as Corporal.
Hixon, Charles		Aug. 19	
Kerby, Edward F		Aug. 19	
Kerby, John F		Aug. 19	
Keara, James B		Aug. 19	
Landreth, William T		Aug. 19	Mustered out July 19, '65.
Landreth, Theodore		Aug. 19	
Landreth, Thomas A		Aug. 19	
Legg, Benjamin M		Aug. 19	Mustered out July 19. '65.
Lacky, Francis N		Aug. 19	
Lewis, Elijah W		Aug. 19	
Lomax, Laniska		Aug. 19	Mustered out July 19, '65, as Corporal.
Lynn, Samuel D		Aug. 19	
Lynn, Granuville S		Aug. 19	
Lynn, Solomon K		Aug. 19	
Mahan, John B		Aug. 19	
Melvin, Thomas C		Aug. 19	
Miller, Joseph H		Aug. 19	Mustered out July 19, '65.
Morris, Joseph		Aug. 19	" " "
Murray, Abel		Aug. 19	Mustered out July 19, '65, as Corporal.
Martin, Jacob G		Aug. 19	Mustered out July 19, '65.
Murrey, Wesley		Aug. 19	" " "
McIntire, Elijah		Aug. 19	Mustered out Feb. 10, '65.
McDaniels, George		Aug. 19	
McNabb, Hugh		Aug. 19	Transferred to V. R. C., Nov. 30, '64.
Moore, Volney T		Aug. 19	Mustered out July 19, '65.
Moyer, Alfred		Aug. 19	" " "
Oldham, George R		Aug. 19	
Pope, Simpson		Aug. 19	
Sloan, Jacob W		Aug. 19	
Smith, George W		Aug. 19	Mustered out July 19, '65.
Snider, James L		Aug. 19	Mustered out May 9, '65.
Sperlin, Hiram		Aug. 19	
Steward, Linsey		Aug. 19	
Starkey, William		Aug. 19	
Tallbott, William B		Aug. 19	Mustered out July 19, '65.
Tomlinson, Henry		Aug. 19	
Tomlinson, William		Aug. 19	
Turner, Oliver		Aug. 19	
Williams, John T		Aug. 19	Mustered out May 14, '65.
Wright, Temple S		Aug. 19	
Recruits.			
Higgins, Cornelius		Jan. 26, '64	Transf'd to Co. "D," 24th Reg't, July 13, '65.
Huff, Elwan B		Nov. 23, '64	" " " "
Hammersley, Frederick		Feb. 29, '65	" " " "
Biddle, Isaac		Jan. 26, '64	" " " "

ENLISTED MEN OF COMPANY "L"

Name and Rank.	Residence.	Date of Muster. 1862.	Remarks.
First Sergeant.			
Carmichael, Joseph F		Aug. 20	
Sergeants.			
Friedly, William W		Aug. 20	Promoted 2d Lieutenant.
Rhoads, Jehial A		Aug. 20	Mustered out July 19, '65, as private.
Brocke, Richard H		Aug. 20	
McCalip, Fieldon		Aug. 20	
Corporals.			
Riley, Charles		Aug. 20	Mustered out July 19, '65, as Sergeant.
Blankenbaker, Reuben A		Aug. 20	Mustered out July 19, '65.
Israel, James		Aug. 20	
Arkuckle, Ephraim		Aug. 20	
Laugh, William J		Aug. 20	Discharged; disability.
Stucker, Isaac		Aug. 20	Mustered out July 19, '65.

Name and Rank.	Residence.	Date of Muster. 1862.	Remarks.
Anderson, John B.		Aug. 20	Mustered out July 19, '65.
Homalay, Christopher		Aug. 20	" " "
Musicians.			
Allen, Benjamin F.		Aug. 20	Mustered out July 19, '65.
Bruner, George W.		Aug. 20	
Wagoner.			
Brown, Matthew		Aug. 20	Discharged June 3, '65; disability.
Privates.			
Banks, John		Aug. 20	Mustered out July 19, '65.
Bannon, Charles L.		Aug. 20	" " "
Bannon, Frederick E.		Aug. 20	" " "
Bietel, Franklin M.		Aug. 20	
Billard, Owen		Aug. 20	Mustered out July 19, '65.
Birchfield, William H.		Aug. 20	
Burk, Bartimus		Aug. 20	Mustered out July 19, '65, as Corporal.
Burcham, John		Aug. 20	
Blair, William		Aug. 20	Mustered out July 19, '65.
Bruner, Henry		Aug. 20	
Bruner, Augustus		Aug. 20	Mustered out July 19, '65.
Case, Henry		Aug. 20	" " "
Casteel, James		Aug. 20	Mustered out May 18, '65.
Cook, Charles S.		Aug. 20	
Covert, William A.		Aug. 20	Mustered out July 19, '65.
Covert, John H.		Aug. 20	" " "
Covert, John W.		Aug. 20	
Clark, John		Aug. 20	Transferred Co., "E" 124th Reg't, July 12,'6
Crisler, John A.		Aug. 20	Mustered out July 19, '65, as Sergeant.
Davis, Harrison W.		Aug. 20	Mustered out July 19, '65.
Dealy, John		Aug. 20	" " "
Dee Gauno, Gerret S.		Aug. 20	
Dudley, Elijah		Aug. 20	
Eaton, Thomas V.		Aug. 20	Mustered out July 19, '65, as 1st Sergeant.
Everet, William C.		Aug. 20	
Edwards, Aquilla		Aug. 20	Mustered out July 19, '65.
Fishel, Calvin F.		Aug. 20	
Fox, Isaac M.		Aug. 20	
Gambold, John		Aug. 20	
Hall, John		Aug. 20	
Houser, Richard		Aug. 20	Mustered out July 19, '65.
Hedgecock, Lewis		Aug. 20	" " "
Hedgecock, John		Aug. 20	
Hedrick, George D.		Aug. 20	
Henry, Roderick		Aug. 20	
Hise, Lewis		Aug. 20	
Bininger, Christopher		Aug. 20	Mustered out July 19, '65
Holland, Leander H.		Aug. 20	
Lawless, Mason		Aug. 20	
Lawrence, John W.		Aug. 20	Mustered out July 19, '65.
Lewis, Michael		Aug. 20	
Lick, Parmenius H.		Aug. 20	
Maddex, William F.		Aug. 20	
Mobley, James		Aug. 20	
McCalip, Hugh		Aug. 20	
McCracken, Nace B.		Aug. 20	
Nelegh, Clinton		Aug. 20	
Reed, Charles A.		Aug. 20	Mustered out July 19, '65.
Reed, Ezra		Aug. 20	" " "
Reed, John A.		Aug. 20	
Reed, William H.		Aug. 20	Mustered out July 19, '65.
Rominger, Thomas		Aug. 20	" " "
Rhorer, Benton		Aug. 20	" " "
Sawers, Emanuel		Aug. 20	
Showalter, William		Aug. 20	
Shults, Henry F.		Aug. 20	Mustered out July 19, '65.
Shutt, Jacob F.		Aug. 20	
Shultz, Irwin S.		Aug. 20	
Skinner, Sanford L.		Aug. 20	
Smith, Charles E.		Aug. 20	Mustered out July 19, '65.
Snyder, Charles H.		Aug. 20	" " "
Snyder, Philip		Aug. 20	
Snyder, Levi		Aug. 20	Mustered out July 19, '65.
Stewart, Robert		Aug. 20	Mustered out July 19, '65, as Sergeant.
Stobs, John		Aug. 20	
Webster, Samuel P.		Aug. 20	Mustered out July 19, '65.
Webster, William M.		Aug. 20	
Zigler, Eli		Aug. 20	Mustered out July 19, '65.

Name and Rank.	Residence.	Date of Muster.	Remarks.
Recruits.			
Anderson, Charles		Feb. 4, '64	Mustered out June 3, '65. [June 29, '65.
Clauder, Henry T		Sept. 31, '62	Transf'd to V. R. C. Dec. 1, '64; muster'd out
Cookson, George W		Nov. 1, '64	Transf'd to Co. "E," 24th Reg't July 13, '65.
Fox, Francis M		Nov. 1, '64	Mustered out June 24, '65.
Gambold, Joseph		Aug. 31, '62	Mustered out June 15, '65.
Hill, Nehemiah		Feb. 4, '64	Mustered out July 12. '65.
Hiner, Joseph J		Jan. 2, '64	Died at Baton Rouge, La., Dec. 25, '64.
Metzger, William		Jan. 27, '64	Transf'd to Co. "E," 24th Reg't, July 13, '65.
Neligh, Clinton		Jan. 27, '64	" " " "
Neligh, Solon		Jan. 27, '64	" " " "
Patterson, Joseph A		Oct. 30, '63	" " " "
Rhodes, Henry H		Jan. 2, '64	Mustered out June 10, '65.
Sanders, Nahum		Jan. 28, '64	Mustered out June 3, '65.
West, Samuel C		Jan. 26, '64	Mustered out June 17, '65.

ENLISTED MEN OF COMPANY "K."

Name and Rank.	Residence.	Date of Muster. 1862.	Remarks.
First Sergeant.			
Robinson, Gabriel		Aug. 20	Promoted 2nd Lieutenant.
Sergeants.			
Lowell, Oscar F		Aug. 20	Promoted 1st Lieutenant.
Findley, George		Aug. 20	
Callihan, Robert		Aug. 20	Promoted 2nd Lieutenant.
Huddleson, James P		Aug. 20	
Corporals.			
Nilson, Alex. N		Aug. 20	Mustered out May 16, '65.
Hancock, William B		Aug. 20	
Crobt, Adam		Aug. 20	
Isaacs, Simpson		Aug. 20	
Graham, Aaron A		Aug. 20	Mustered out May 16, '65.
Ramy, George T		Aug. 20	
Robertson, Joseph		Aug. 20	
Johnson, George W		Aug. 20	Mustered out July 19, '65.
Musicians.			
Johnson, Isaac		Aug. 20	
Lockasur, Francis M		Aug. 20	Mustered out July 19, '65.
Wagoner.			
Phifer, John		Aug. 20	
Privates.			
Barkman, William M		Aug. 20	
Beezley, Charles C		Aug. 20	
Bland, John K		Aug. 20	Mustered out July 19, '65.
Bland, Meredith		Aug. 20	Mustered out May 31, '65.
Brown, Jacob		Aug. 20	
Brown, James A		Aug. 20	
Brown, Amos D		Aug. 20	
Casey, Presley		Aug. 20	
Claycamp, John C		Aug. 20	
Claycamp, Henry H		Aug. 20	
Claycamp, John F		Aug. 20	
Compton, David		Aug. 20	Mustered out July 5, '65.
Cornett, Archibald		Aug. 20	
Cross, Levi M		Aug. 20	Mustered out June 25, '65.
Cone, Marcellus		Aug. 20	Mustered out July 19, '65.
Comby, Silas		Aug. 20	
Coulter, John A		Aug. 20	
Dunlap, Robert Mc		Aug. 20	Mustered out July 19, '65.
Findley, Gabriel M		Aug. 20	
Fisher, Daniel B		Aug. 20	Mustered out July 19, '65; Corp'l.
Fleetwood, Washington		Aug. 20	Discharged Jan. 30, '65; disability.
Flinn, John		Aug. 20	Mustered out July 19, '65.
Foster, David J		Aug. 20	" " "
George, John		Aug. 20	" " "
Goldsmith, Russell H		Aug. 20	
Grayson, John		Aug. 20	Mustered out July 19, '65.
Gudgill, Shelby G		Aug. 20	" " "
Goldsmith, Milbrin H		Aug. 20	" " "
Guffey, Charles		Aug. 20	

139

Name and Rank.	Residence.	Date of Muster 1862.	Remarks.
Hancock, James		Aug. 20	
Hannah, Abner W		Aug. 20	Mustered out July 19, '65
Haney, Erasmus N		Aug. 20	Mustered out July 19, '65, as Corporal.
Hinkle, James A		Aug. 20	Mustered out July 19, '65, as Sergeant.
Hood, Wyatt		Aug. 20	
Hood, Robert		Aug. 20	
Hood, John S		Aug. 20	Mustered out July 19, '65.
Huffington, James W		Aug. 20	" "
Isaacs, William Mc		Aug. 20	
Jackson, James D		Aug. 20	
Jones, Henry		Aug. 20	
Jones, Robert G		Aug. 20	
Kindred, Marion R		Aug. 20	Discharged May 23, '65; disability.
Kolb, Andrew		Aug. 20	
Langdon, George, Jr		Aug. 20	Mustered out July 19, '65.
Lilton, Morgan M		Aug. 20	
Lorens, John		Aug. 20	
McHayne, William D		Aug. 20	Mustered out July 19, '65, as Sergeant.
McHayne, Thomas E		Aug. 20	
McMillen, Joseph		Aug. 20	
Newby, Lawrence D		Aug. 20	
Nelson, John H		Aug. 20	
Parker, Christopher		Aug. 20	
Pate, Hartwell		Aug. 20	
Payne, James		Aug. 20	Mustered out July 19, '65.
Peters, Jesse B		Aug. 20	
Plummer, Alexander C		Aug. 20	
Prince, Thomas G		Aug. 20	
Pruden, James		Aug. 20	
Pruitt, Richard		Aug. 20	Mustered out July 19, '65.
Richards, Thomas Z		Aug. 20	
Rich, Jacob		Aug. 20	Mustered out July 19, '65.
Roberts, Benjamin F		Aug. 20	" "
Roberts, W. M		Aug. 20	
Ross, Charles P		Aug. 20	Discharged by order War Dep't, Aug. 26, '64.
Ruder, Samuel M		Aug. 20	
Smith, John		Aug. 20	Mustered out July 19, '65.
Smith, James M		Aug. 20	
Sturling, Hanson		Aug. 20	Mustered out July 19, '65.
Stark, Elijah		Aug. 20	
Stafford, John L		Aug. 20	Mustered out July 19, '65.
Stafford, John H		Aug. 20	" "
Stockwell, David A		Aug. 20	Mustered out July 19, '65, as Corporal.
Summa, Frederick		Aug. 20	
Sutton, William N		Aug. 20	
Taber, Granville		Aug. 20	
Taylor, James B		Aug. 20	
Waddle, Charles		Aug. 20	Mustered out June 6, '64.
Weekly, Wesly B		Aug. 20	Mustered out July 19, '65.
Wheeler, Alonzo C		Aug. 20	
Wilkie, Hosea C		Aug. 20	Mustered out July 19, '65.
Wyman, Francis		Aug. 20	
Wilson, John		Aug. 20	Discharged Feb. 16, '65; disability; Serg't.
Wirner, Francis N		Aug. 20	Mustered out July 19, '65, as absent sick.
Recruits.			
Bland, Henry L		March 4, '64	Discharged June 3, '65; disability.
Bowman, John H		March 1, '64	Discharged July 11, '65; disability.
Day, William M		April 5, '64	Transferred Co. "C," 24th Reg't, July 13, '65.
Perry, William		April 5, '64	Mustered out June 5, '65.
Perry, Joseph		March 4, '64	Transf'd to Co. "C," 24th Reg't, July 13, '65.

UNASSIGNED RECRUITS.

Name and Rank.	Residence.	Date of Muster.	Remarks.
Douglass, George W		Jan. 2, '64	
Dorst, Frank		Jan. 12, '64	
Graham, Aaron A		Aug. 12, '62	
Hill, James		July 24, '62	
Harian, William		Jan. 17, '64	
Henderson, Charles		Feb. 22, '64	
Hendrixson, Stiles H		Jan. 4, '64	
Johnson, Lewis W		Jan. 4, '64	
Lynch, William H		Jan. 20, '64	

Name and Rank.	Residence.	Date of Muster	Remarks.
Richardson, Samuel	....	Feb. 22, '64	
Shutz, Henry S.....	....	July 21, '62	
Shuck, George......	....	Jan. 24, '64	
Vannorman, Seldon	....	Jan. 28, '64	
Winters, William..	....	July 24, '62	

www.ingramcontent.com/pod-product-compliance
Lightning Source LLC
Chambersburg PA
CBHW030435190426
43202CB00036B/1129